THE CEL

'Having read Helen Litton's excellent books on the Famine and the Civil War, I am pleased that she has now turned her pen to the Celts to provide an attractive, informative and inexpensive text for the general reader.' *Dr Barry Raftery, Associate Professor of Archaeology at University College, Dublin.*

CHRONOLOGY

TIMELINE	EUROPE	BRITAIN	IRELAND
8th – 7th centuries BC	Late Bronze Age (Hallstatt A and B) Early Iron Age (Hallstatt C and D), the first Celts	Bronze Age	Bronze Age
7th – 5th centuries BC	Hecataeus makes reference to 'Celts' La Tène Iron Age	Hallstatt Iron Age	Hallstatt Iron Age (traces)
5th – 3rd centuries BC	Herodotus makes reference to 'Celts' 390 BC Celts sack Rome 325 BC Change to 'P-Celtic' has taken place 290 BC Celts sack Delphi	250 BC La Tène Iron Age –	250 BC La Tène Iron Age – Celts arrive [?]
3rd – 1st centuries BC	La Tène culture declines	British contacts with Belgae 100 BC Belgic tribes arrive 52 BC Julius Caesar defeats Gauls 55 BC Julius Caesar invades 43 BC Emperor Claudius invades	100 BC British tribes arrive [?]
1st century AD	Calendar of Coligny		Roman material
2nd century AD	Ptolemy's *Geography*		

THE CELTS

An Illustrated History

Helen Litton

Picture Research Peter Costello

WOLFHOUND PRESS

First published 1997 by
WOLFHOUND PRESS Ltd
68 Mountjoy Square
Dublin 1

British Library Cataloguing in Publication Data
A catalogue record for this book is available from the British Library

ISBN 0-86327-577-X

The publishers have made every reasonable effort to contact the copyright holders
of material reproduced in this book. If any involuntary infringement of copyright has
occurred, sincere apologies are offered and the owners of such copyright are
requested to contact the publishers.

Cover design: Slick Fish Design, Dublin
Cover photograph: Bronze horse-mask from Stanwick, England. Height 101mm.
AKG London, by Erich Lessing
Typesetting: Wolfhound Press
Printed in the Republic of Ireland by Colour Books, Dublin

PREFACE

The whole question of the Irish Iron Age, and the relationship of the Celts to it, is very confused, but I have tried to lay out the known facts as clearly as possible. My task was greatly assisted by Dr Barry Raftery, Associate Professor of Archaeology at University College, Dublin, who was most helpful with advice and illustrations. Any errors are, of course, my responsibility alone. Dr Máire Delaney, lecturer in the Department of Anatomy, Trinity College Dublin, willingly shared her expertise on bog bodies. I am extremely grateful for the access to the resources of the National Library of Ireland, The Central Catholic Library, and the Royal Society of Antiquaries of Ireland.

Finally, along with my acknowledgements to Seamus Cashman, Susan Houlden and the staff of Wolfhound Press, I must give special mention to Peter Costello, who carried out the onerous task of picture research with skill and energy, and has been the most valuable contributor to *The Celts: An Illustrated History.*

Helen Litton

1997

Caesar, Pliny, Tacitus, Orosius, and all the Latin writers call it [Ireland] Hibernia. The etymology of this name is thought to be uncertain. Some think it is derived from the Iberians, a people of Spain, who occupied the island; or from the river Iberus in Spain, or from Iberia, the ancient name of Spain itself. But others derive it from Heber, one of the sons of Milesius, or from Heremon his brother.

The island was known to the English during six or seven centuries by the name of Ireland. Of this name the etymology is evident, and explains itself; it means the land of Ir, the first Milesian prince who came over from Spain to explore the country...

Immediately before the arrival of the Milesians it was called Eire, Fodla, and Banba, from three queens of that name who married three brothers, monarchs of Ireland. These brothers reigned by turns, a year each. But the name Eire always was and still is most in use, the inhabitants being at this day known by the name of Eirinachts or natives of Eire, in Latin Erigena.

A New and Impartial History of Ireland from the Earliest Accounts to the Present Time by M. McDermot, London, 1823.

THE CELTS
INTRODUCTION

Ireland, a small island on the western periphery of the continent of Europe, is popularly supposed to preserve the traditions of the ancient, powerful and widely-spread group of tribes called, in the ancient world, the Celts. Celtic survivals are known in other parts of western Europe, but those are the remains of cultures shattered by the Roman Conquest, and the later barbaric invasions. Ireland, isolated from European events once Britain was invaded by Rome, alone maintained its Celtic heritage, untouched, until the coming of Christianity.

At any rate, this is the carefully-crafted image of Ireland, beloved of the tourist board and of creative artists seeking a cultural context apart from the mainstream. This image gave Ireland a much-needed sense of individual identity, and kept hope of independence alive, through centuries of British domination. But the image relies heavily on the romantic imaginings of seventeenth, eighteenth and nineteenth century antiquarians, who began to examine old Irish texts which had been neglected for centuries. Wrestling with a language which few of them understood, and building extraordinary theories out of garbled sentences, they constructed a 'Celtic Twilight', a story of the survival of ancient lore and noble qualities which had been lost everywhere else. The Irish Celts were seen as mystical, brooding, fey, in touch with the supernatural, impossible for the down-to-earth, commonsensical Anglo-Saxons to comprehend.

These antiquarians were not the first to build up a misleading picture. Early medieval Irish historians had used the annual records kept in monasteries (known as 'annals'), combined with ancient myths and legends, to create a history of Ireland as one nation, populated solely by Celts. Every important tribe was given a clear line of descent from a legendary founder-figure. The technique of 'euhemerism' was widely used: this means that the names of mythical gods were given to human beings, depriving the gods of their divine characteristics and setting them firmly in a human context. This helped to cover up the shameful fact that the Irish had once worshipped pagan gods.

Two-faced idol, Celtic style, undated, Boa Island, Don Sutton Photo Library.

One of the earliest of such texts is *Lebor Gabála*, The Book of the Takings (or 'Invasions'). It was probably begun in the seventh or eighth century AD, but only survives in a twelfth century manuscript. It was read as incontrovertible fact by seventeenth century scholars such as Geoffrey Keating. According to this book, the first invasion of Ireland was led by a man called Partholon, but his tribe died of a plague, leaving no descendants at all. The next invasion was led by Nemed mac Agnomain, whose people were attacked by the Fomoire or Formorians (the indigenous inhabitants), and finally left the country again. A son of Nemed is supposed to have gone to Britain, and become ancestor to all the Britons.

The first people, then...are known as 'Formorians'. As far as we can gather, they were a dark, low-browed, stunted race...a race of utterly savage hunters and fishermen, ignorant of metal, of pottery, possibly even of the use of fire; using the stone hammers and hatchets of which vast numbers remain in Ireland to this day...Perhaps if we think of the Lapps of the present day, and picture them wandering about the country, catching the hares and rabbits in nooses, burrowing in the earth or amongst rocks, and being, not impossibly, looked down on with scorn by the great Irish elk which still stalked majestically over the hills; rearing ugly little altars to dim, formless gods; trembling at every sudden gust, and seeing demon faces in every bush and brake, it will give us a fairly good notion of what these very earliest inhabitants of Ireland were probably like.

The Story of the Nations – Ireland, by Hon Emily Lawless,
London, 1889.

Three more tribes, called the Fir Bolg, the Galioin and the Domnainn, then settled in Ireland. They were overcome by the Erainn who came from Britain, led by Lugaid, a descendant of the god Daire. Other invaders were the Tuatha De Danann and the

Milesians, 'Sons of Mil', from Spain, who were also called 'Scoti'. The leaders of the Tuatha De Danann bear the names of various Celtic gods; later legends turned them into fairy people, who lived underground. The Milesians or Scoti, the final prehistoric invaders, were therefore in this version of events the actual Celts, coming to Ireland for the first time about 400 years BC, overcoming all other inhabitants.

Nothing of the foregoing is reliable historical fact. The people who wrote this type of pseudo-history acted as public relations officers for one tribal grouping or another, and were trying to prove how noble their tribe's ancestry was, and how long-established its supremacy. They used legend, myth, poetry, names of gods and fairies, fragments of literature written down centuries after its original composition, and mixed a potent brew. Most of these tales are a special pleading of one kind or another, with perfectly understandable motives behind them. Historical accuracy was not the point. But these stories were still being told as historical fact up to the early twentieth century, in school history-books, and have left their mark.

In the eighteenth and nineteenth centuries, as Irish nationalism began to grow and develop, it became important to challenge the idea that the ancient Celts were barbaric pagans who had had to be civilised, first by Christianity, and later by the Anglo-Normans. Learned antiquarians, English, Irish and Anglo-Irish, quarrelled violently over the evidence provided by megalithic tombs, round towers, mythological tales, Old Irish law tracts and bardic poetry, trying to fit the ancient Irish into one pigeon-hole or another. Pseudo-philologists linked the Irish language, tortuously, with Etruscan, but finally the connection with Welsh was made, and for the first time the Irish Celts were provided with a European background.

Numerous theories, one wilder than the next, were put forward for Celtic origins. The ancient Irish were said to be descended from the primitive Scyths of Scythia (because it sounded like 'Scoti'), and the Scyths themselves were traced back to Japhet, son of Noah.

Alternatively, the Celts were said to have come from the Middle East, from a much more developed and sophisticated Phoenician civilisation. Naturally, scholars who believed that the English were the source of all civilisation tended to favour the Scytho-Celtic theory, refusing to allow any good qualities to the primitive Irish.

As Joep Leerssen outlines in his studies on Irish nationalism, a more subtle point was made by scholars such as Samuel Ferguson, who decided that the true Celts were those who had been responsible for the Irish megalithic tombs, and the technical brilliance of Irish bronze age metalwork. This, of course, meant that the brutal Milesians, who brought iron and exterminated the existing population, had had no better right to rule Ireland than the later Anglo-Normans, because they were merely conquerors themselves. Therefore they could not claim any superior right to own the country now.

> When Hibernians compare their present with their former condition, their just and equal laws, with those that were uncertain and capricious; the happy security of peace with the miseries of barbarous manners, their hearts must overflow with gratitude to the Author of such blessings; nor will they deny their obligations to the fostering care of Britain, the happy instrument for conferring them.
>
> Introduction, *Antiquities of Ireland*, by Edward Ledwich, Dublin, 1804.

As the nineteenth century progressed, the wilder theories were exploded. Scholars such as George Petrie and John O'Donovan brought scientific analysis to bear on Irish texts and antiquities, and a more soundly-based picture of prehistoric Ireland began to emerge. Archaeological techniques were developed, and proper excavations began to replace the random, destructive diggings such as those of the British Israelites, who searched for the Ark of the Covenant on the Hill of Tara and destroyed irrecoverable evidence in the process. Philologists studied the roots of the Irish language, and Old Irish became better understood. Scholarly analysis of monastic, poetic and annalistic texts began to provide a clearer picture of dating and chronology.

But the romantic Celtic Twilight dies hard. Brought into the popular perception by writers such as W B Yeats and Lady Gregory, and immortalised in song by Thomas Moore and others, the image of the mystical, close-to-nature, talking-to-the-fairies Celt became more influential than ever towards the close of the nineteenth century and the beginning of the twentieth. This was when Irish militant nationalism was reaching its height, and the Celtic Twilight provided a series of shorthand references, understood by everyone, which harked back to noble forefathers maintaining an ancient culture (and Catholicism too, of course) against dungeon, fire and sword.

It was extremely important, politically, to emphasise difference, to appeal to Ireland's past as a mark for a free and independent future. The term 'Celtic' implied all that was *not* British, *not* Roman, *not* Anglo-Saxon, *not* Germanic. It linked Ireland with other groupings that equally proclaimed their independence on the grounds of difference – the Scots, the Welsh, the Bretons, the Basques. But did the whole idea have any real validity? That is what this book hopes to explore.

Above: *Thomas Moore, whose poems and songs helped to create a Romantic notion of early Ireland (from* The Cabinet of Irish Literature, *1898).*

Right: *William Butler Yeats leader of the literary movement that promoted the idea of 'the Celtic Twilight' (from* The Cabinet of Irish Literature, *1898).*

Above: *An idealised Early Gaelic homestead. Courtesy Peter Costello.*
Left: *The Red-Branch Knights of Ulster, riding into battle in a chariot. Courtesy Peter Costello.*
Below: *The three classes of Ireland: the High King with his druid and bard. Courtesy Peter Costello.*

Fanciful idea of ancient Celtic warrior (which owes more to Wagner than archaeology), from a Dublin publication of 1906. Courtesy Peter Costello.

Left: *The fate of King Daithi. From* Irish Songs And Ballads, *edited by John Boyle O'Reilly (Boston 1888).*

Opposite: *The death of Cuchulain, champion of Ulster, defending his province against the southern invaders, as recounted in* The Táin. *1916 Memorial in the G.P.O., Dublin. Photograph Bord Fáilte – The Irish Trade Board .*

Below: *The triumph of the Gaels over the native inhabitants of Ireland, in the schoolbook version of Irish history. Courtesy Peter Costello.*

Long, long ago, beyond the misty space
Of twice a thousand years,
In Erin old there dwelt a mighty race,
Taller than Roman spears;
Like oaks and towers they had a giant grace,
Were fleet as deers,
With wind and waves they made their 'biding place,
These western shepherd seers.

Their Ocean-God was Manannan MacLir,
Whose angry lips,
In their white foam, full often would inter
Whole fleets of ships;
Cromah their Day-God, and their Thunderer
Made morning and eclipse;
Bride was their Queen of Song, and unto her
They prayed with fire-touched lips.

Great were their deeds, their passions and their sports;
With clay and stone
They piled on strath and shore those mystic forts,
Not yet o'erthrown;
On cairn-crowned hills they held their council-courts;
While youths alone,
With giant dogs, explored the elk resorts,
And brought them down.

Thomas D'Arcy Magee
(1825-68).

1

IRON AGE EUROPE

The Celts of western Europe, a prehistoric people, entered the historic record through the written accounts of Greeks and Romans who had dealings with them. Since they did not develop literacy themselves, they have left no history of their own; what we are told about them was mostly recorded by people who thought of them as primitive, brutal or childish.

We know from the archaeological record that the Celts originated in central and east-central Europe, about the mid-eighth century BC, in what is known as the Early Iron Age. They seem to

---

Nearly all the Gauls are of a lofty stature, fair and of ruddy complexion: terrible from the sternness of their eyes, very quarrelsome, and of great pride and insolence. A whole troup of foreigners would not be able to withstand a single Gaul if he called his wife to his assistance who is usually very strong and with blue eyes; especially when, swelling her neck, gnashing her teeth, and brandishing her sallow arms of enormous size, she begins to strike blows mingled with kicks, as if they were so many missiles sent from the string of a catapult.

AMMIANUS MARCELLINUS (sixth century AD, copying Timagenes, who wrote between 63 BC and 14 AD. Ammianus Marcellinus was a Roman historian, who compiled a massive history of the Roman empire.

represent a coming together of various groups, during the Bronze Age, who gradually developed a single culture around the discovery and use of iron. They were called 'Galli' or 'Galatae' by the Romans, and 'Keltoi' by the Greeks, but we do not know what they called themselves, or how homogenous they were. Groups called 'Celtic' gradually spread south and east, occupying Spain, Italy and the area around the Danube, driven by a growing population and the need for more farmland. Eventually, groups reached Britain and Ireland.

The whole nation that is nowadays called Gallic or Galatic is war-mad, and both high-spirited and quick for battle, although otherwise simple and not uncouth. Because of this, if the Gauls are provoked they tend to rush into a battle all together, without concealment or forward planning. For anyone who wants to outwit them they are therefore easy to deal with, since it is enough to provoke them into a rage by any means at all, at any time and in any place. It will then be found that they are willing to risk everything they have with nothing to rely on other than their sheer physical strength and courage. If gentle persuasion is used, however, they will readily apply themselves to useful things such as education and the art of speaking. Their strength is due partly to their size – for they are large – and partly to their numbers...

In addition to their simplicity and exuberance the Gauls have a propensity for empty-headed boasting and have a passion for personal ornamentation. They wear a lot of gold; they put golden collars around their necks and bracelets on their arms and wrists, while dignitaries wear dyed or stained clothing that is spangled with gold. Their vanity therefore makes them unbearable in victory, while defeat plunges them into deepest despair. Their thoughtlessness is also accompanied by traits of barbarity and savagery, as is so often the case with the population of the north.

STRABO, Geography, IV, 4.2, 5
Strabo was a Greek geographer
whose *Geographica*, in seventeen volumes,
is of enormous value to classical scholars.

...Their swords are as long as the javelins of other peoples, and their javelins have points longer than swords. Some of their javelins are forged with a straight head, while some are spiral with breaks throughout their entire length so that the blow not only cuts but also tears the flesh, and the recovery of the spear tears open the wound.

DIODORUS SICULUS (First century BC)
World History, V.28,30.
Born in Sicily. Spent thirty years collecting material
for *History of the World* in forty volumes.
At least fifteen volumes survive.

Romans fighting Celts in a chariot. Woodcut from Caesar's Gallic Wars *by Bruno Bramanti.*

It was their custom when drawn up for battle to come forward before the front line and challenge the bravest of their enemies drawn up opposite them to single combat. Whenever one accepts the challenge, they praise in song the manly virtues of their ancestors and also their own brave deeds...Then reviling and belittling their opponents they try to rob them by their words of their boldness of spirit before the contest.

DIODORUS SICULUS (First century BC)

Above left: *Roman soldier, woodcut by Bruno Bramanti.*
Above right: *Close battle of Celts and Romans, woodcut by Bruno Bramanti.*

The Gauls are tall, with moist white flesh; their hair is not only naturally blond, but they also make artificial efforts to lighten its colour by washing it frequently in lime water. They pull it back from the top of the head to the nape of the neck...Thanks to this treatment their hair thickens until it is just like a horse's mane. Some shave their beards, others let them grow moderately; nobles keep their cheeks clean-shaven but let their moustaches grow long until they cover their mouths...They wear amazing clothes: tunics dyed in every colour and trousers that they call *bracae* (breeches). They pin striped cloaks on top, of thick cloth in winter and light material in summer, decorated with small, densely packed, multi-coloured squares.

DIODORUS SICULUS (First century BC),

Warrior with headgear. Stone figure from Hirschlanden (late 6th – early 5th BC). Height 150cm. Württembergisches Landesmuseum, Stuttgart, Germany. Photograph AKG London, by Erich Lessing.

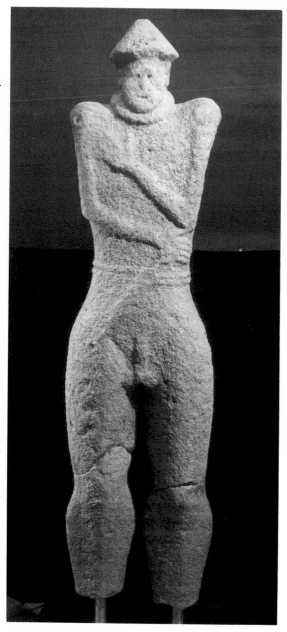

Physically the Celts are terrifying in appearance, with deep-sounding and very harsh voices. In conversation they use few words and speak in riddles, for the most part hinting at things and leaving a great deal to be understood. They frequently exaggerate with the aim of extolling themselves and diminishing the status of others. They are boasters and threateners and given to bombastic self-dramatisation, and yet they are quick of mind and with good natural ability for learning. They have also lyric poets whom they call Bards. They sing to the accompaniment of instruments resembling lyres, sometimes a eulogy and sometimes a satire.

DIODORUS SICULUS (First century BC)

They have also certain philosophers and theologians who are treated with special honour, whom they call Druids. They further make use of seers, thinking them worthy of high praise. These latter by their augural observances and by the sacrifice of sacrificial animals can foretell the future and they hold all the people subject to them. In particular, when enquiring into matters of great import, they have a strange and incredible custom; they devote to death a human being and stab him with a dagger in the region above the diaphragm, and when he has fallen they foretell the future from his fall and from the convulsions of his limbs and, moreover, from the spurting of the blood, placing their trust in some ancient and long-continued observation of these practices.

DIODORUS SICULUS (First century BC)

*Defeated Celts,
woodcut by
Bruno Bramanti.*

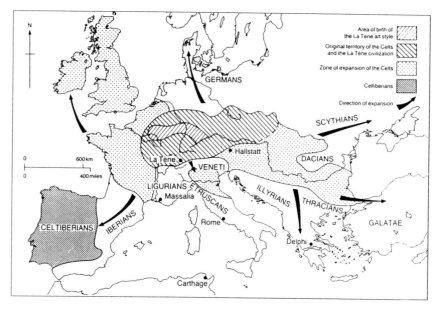

The territories occupied by Celts from the fifth century BC until the Roman conquest. (From The Celtic World, *Miranda Green, Routledge, 1995. After R. and V Megaw,* Celtic Art, *Thames and Hudson, 1989.)*

Early mentions of the Celts are found in the work of Hecataeus of Miletus (late sixth century BC), and the fifth century BC writer Herodotus also mentions them. They were fierce opponents, even against trained armies; they sacked Rome about 387 BC, after the Roman republic tried to help the Etruscans of northern Italy against them, and the Romans feared and hated the Celts ever after. Roughly one hundred years later, they sacked Delphi, the most holy shrine in Greece, but were eventually driven off.

As the Roman Empire expanded, the Celts were driven from adjoining countries, and also found themselves under pressure from neighbouring Germanic tribes. By the end of the second century BC their power had declined. On the continent, their area of influence became reduced to Gaul (modern France), where Julius Caesar conquered them in the first century BC. Most of the accounts we have of them date from this period of decline.

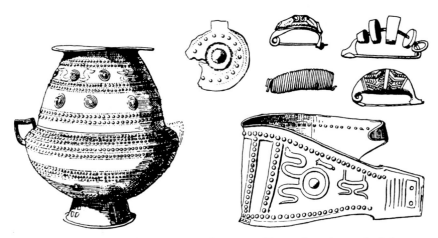

Italian Urnfield types: bronze ossuary for cremated bones, brooches, and a belt-plate from a tomb at Monterozzi, Corneto. After Montelius.

...Since the qualities of the climate are spoiled by the excess of cold, the land [Gaul] bears neither wine nor oil, and therefore the Gauls, being deprived of these fruits, concoct a drink out of barley called *zythos* (beer), and they wash honeycombs and use the washings as a drink. They are exceedingly fond of wine, and sate themselves with the unmixed wine imported by merchants; their desire makes them drink it greedily and when they become drunk they fall into a stupor or into a maniacal disposition. And therefore many Italian merchants with their usual love of lucre look on the Gallic love of wine as their treasure trove.

DIODORUS SICULUS (First century BC)

Although their wives are beautiful, they pay very little attention to them, but rather have a strange passion for the embraces of males. Their custom is to sleep on the ground upon the skins of wild animals and to wallow among bedfellows on each side. The strangest thing of all is that without a thought of keeping up proper appearances they carelessly yield their virginity to others, and this they regard not as a disgrace, but rather think themselves slighted when someone refuses to accept their freely offered favours.

DIODORUS SICULUS (First century BC)

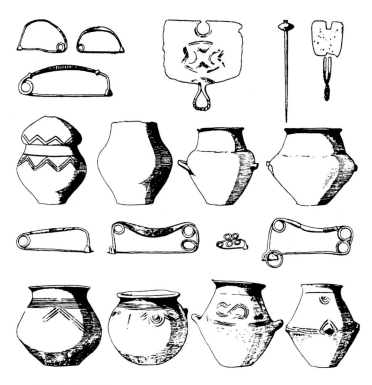

Italian Urnfield types: brooches, razors and urns, from Timmari, Apulia, and Pianello. After Gordon Childe.

Material Culture

For archaeologists, the term 'material culture' covers everything used by a particular group of people, such as their weaponry, houses, jewellery and burial rites. The later Bronze Age culture of central and northern Europe is called the 'Urnfield' culture after the method of burial, which was cremation, in pots, in flat cemeteries or urnfields. Dating from the late second millennium BC, this culture excelled in metal technology, manufacturing thin sheets of bronze for such uses as armour and shields. Some scholars think of the

*Grave of the Celtic chieftain found at Hochdorf, near Stuttgart, in 1878.
After Jorg Biel.*

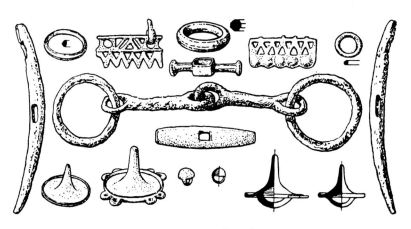

*Horse gear from Beratzhausen, with Hallstatt bit.
After Gordon Childe.*

Urnfield people as 'proto-Celts', as they lived in much the same
areas as the Celts later did.

From about the twelfth century BC, a new material culture
developed, characterised by horse-riding warriors with long
slashing swords, some of which were made of iron. This culture is

*The design
traditions of the
Celts: Aylesford
and (right)
La Tène.
Coffey catalogue.*

*Bronze disk
(restored) typical
of La Tène style.
Coffey catalogue.*

called 'Hallstatt', after a huge cemetery in Austria which marked the centre of a salt-mining industry, and a massive trading empire. The Hallstatt phase lasted to about 450 BC. Many wealthy burials were found, containing large quantities of battle-gear, wagons, jewellery and so on for the next world.

The Hallstatt phase was followed by the La Tène phase, from about 450 BC. This culture is named for a lakeside site in Switzerland where large quantities of material were found, probably offerings to the gods which were deliberately deposited in the water. The La Tène phase, the late Iron Age, lasted until the Celts began coming in contact with the Roman world, which eventually

Details of metal work from Waldalgesheim find, Germany. Coffey catalogue.

Opposite: *Three wooden figures (1st BC), from the Gallo-Roman cult site at the source of the Seine River, St. Germain sur Seine, France. Musée Archéologique, Dijon, France. Photograph AKG London, by Erich Lessing.*

Examples of the intricate design of Celtic metal work, from south-west Germany Coffey catalogue.

overwhelmed them. The essence of the La Tène culture is its particularly sophisticated use of decorative art, particularly on metalwork. The Celts loved display, and carried their wealth in portable form, such as jewellery or horse-trappings. They used gold plentifully, and the torque, or gold collar, is the form of jewellery most associated with them.

....For they wear bracelets on wrists and arms, and round their necks thick rings of solid gold, and they wear also fine finger-rings and even golden tunics. The Celts of the hinterland have a strange and peculiar custom in connection with the sanctuaries of the gods; for in the temples and sanctuaries which are dedicated throughout the country, a large amount of gold is openly placed as a dedication to the gods, and of the native inhabitants none touch it because of religious veneration, although the Celts are unusually fond of money.

DIODORUS SICULUS (First century BC)

Iron was of supreme importance in enabling the Celts to spread and prosper. It was cheaper and more easily available than bronze, which had been the dominant metal used for swords and tools until then. Metal was no longer only a luxury good. Iron tools could clear forests more efficiently, and iron spears and shields gave the Celts an advantage in battle.

The La Tène Celts buried their dead, accompanied by weapons or ornaments, in large cemeteries. Graves of important warriors, often covered by mounds which marked them as special, contained the dead man lying on his war-chariot, surrounded by warlike gear. Although the enduring image we have of European Celts is of a warrior society, it was basically agricultural. Both pastoral and arable agriculture were practised, depending on the type of soil available. Wooden ploughshares were used, though iron ones were later developed as well.

The European Celts constructed large forts, on hill-top positions, which acted as fortified camps but probably contained dwellings as well. Some of these forts later developed into what were almost towns, or tribal capitals. From other cultures, they borrowed such refinements as the use of coinage, but they never developed a unified and disciplined political system. It is uncertain to what extent the various Celtic groups saw themselves as being related, whatever outside observers thought.

Non-Material Culture

Once they began to come into contact with the classical world, Celts made use of the Greek and Roman alphabets for inscriptions, particularly in Gaul, but they never became properly literate. The language they used was Indo-European in origin, part of a family of languages which stretched across Europe to India – Greek and Latin are also fundamentally Indo-European. The basic Celtic language survives in some placenames and personal names recorded by classical authors, as well as a number of inscriptions (in Spain), graffiti on pottery, and dedications at sacred shrines.

The spread of early Celtic languages may well date back to about the sixth century BC, during the Hallstatt period, although scholars have traditionally associated it with the spread of La Tène culture. As a non-literate society, the Celts placed great value on the ability to speak well and fluently, and their use of language was described by contemporary writers as being highly-coloured and poetic, characterised by boasting and exaggeration.

We know very little about Celtic religion, apart from the remains of a few religious sanctuaries. The human head was of almost sacramental importance; heads were taken as trophies in battle, and many of their shrines contained human skulls, or carved representations of heads. The head was seen as the residence of the soul; taking a man's head implied control of his spirit.

Posidonios (first century BC) mentions druids, bards (or poets) and seers. The seers used augury (reading the entrails of animals) to foretell the future. They are also said to have presided over human sacrifices.

> They embalm in cedar-oil the heads of the most distinguished enemies and preserve them carefully in a chest and display them with pride to strangers saying that for this head one of their ancestors, or his father, or the man himself, refused the offer of a large sum of money. They say that some of them boast that they refused the weight of the head in gold.
>
> DIODORUS SICULUS (First century BC)

Stone doorway of a Celto-Ligurian sanctuary for the exhibition of severed human heads (6th – 1st BC). Reconstruction. Height approximately 300cm. Musée Borely, Marseille, France. Photograph AKG London, by Erich Lessing

There is also that custom, barbarous and exotic, which attends most of the northern tribes...when they depart from the battle they hang the heads of their enemies from the necks of their horses, and when they have brought them home, nail the spectacle to the doors of their houses. At any rate Posidonius says that he himself saw this spectacle in many places, and that, although at first he loathed it, afterwards through his familiarity with it, he could bear it calmly.

STRABO (64 BC – AD 21), *Geography*, IV, 4, 5.

From what little we know of the druids, they seem to have been more teachers than priests, transmitting learning through poetry, which was learned by heart. They were philosophers, studying nature and the universe, and teaching the immortality of the soul, and the transmigration of the soul to another body some time after death. According to Caesar, Gaulish druids were sent to Britain for their training, and it is possible that druidism developed in Britain originally. The Celts of Italy, Spain and some other areas do not seem to have had druids.

None of the druidic teaching was ever written down, and all of it was lost when Caesar finally destroyed their last sanctuaries. However, the Calendar of Coligny, which dates to the first century AD, gives us some information on the Celtic year; the druids were obviously practised in astronomy. This Calendar, found in France in 1897, shows sixteen columns of months covering a period of five years. (Diodorus Siculus (first century BC) tells us that the Celts held major festivals every five years – at which animal sacrifices (and possibly human) were made.) Some months and days are marked 'good' (*mat*) or 'not good' (*anm*, an abbreviation). Festival days are also marked – for example, 'Rivros', the 'great festal month', starts around the first of August, and seems to coincide with the Irish festival 'Lughnasa', which celebrates the god Lugh (see below). Coligny itself is near Lyons, which was originally called Lugdunum, 'fortress of Lugh'.

The druids may also have practised medicine. Skulls have been found which bore evidence of 'trepanning', that is, boring a hole in the skull. Some of these had started to heal, which shows that the patient survived the operation, at least for a time.

The Celts seem to have worshipped various tribal gods, as well as local gods which they came across as they moved west, all under the authority of a few major gods who are dominant wherever the Celts are found. Most of our information about their gods comes from the period after close contacts had been made with the Romans, so we know very little about the earliest forms of Celtic gods. Apparently, the human world was seen to reflect the divine

A boar, bronze statuette (2nd – 1st BC) from a tomb in the Sarka Valley, Bohemia. National Museum, Prague, Czech Republic. Photograph AKG London, by Erich Lessing.

world; for example, conflict among mortals meant that the gods were also fighting in the heavens. The Celts, strictly speaking, did not worship their gods, but treated them more as another tribal group with whom they could interact. Deposits of valuable jewellery and weapons were made as offerings, particularly in 'wetland sites' – lakesides, riverbeds, marshes, wells.

Most of the images of Celtic gods date from the later period of Celtic culture, and imitate Roman religious figures, but some are pre-Roman. Figure-carvings at religious sanctuaries such as Roquepertuse may represent gods, and there is a sculpture of a boar-god from Haute-Marne in France, dating from the second or first century BC. It wears a torc, and a boar is carved on the chest.

Wooden carvings would also have been made, but would not have survived. One of the most important sources for the representation of Celtic deities is the huge silver Gundestrup Cauldron, found in Denmark and dating to the second or first century BC. It seems to have been of Thracian manufacture rather than Celtic, but the symbolism is undoubtedly Celtic. It includes pictures of a wheel-god, a ram-headed snake, and men sacrificing bulls (*see colour section*).

Julius Caesar described the Celtic gods, but in terms of the Roman gods he knew. Late Roman sources give us some Celtic names for various gods, such as Teutates, Esus and Taranis. There were also various gods of healing, and mother-goddesses, probably representing fertility. The gods which occur most frequently throughout the Celtic world are listed below.

TARANIS, the thunder-god, is sometimes identified with the Roman Jupiter, ruler of the gods. Jupiter is also linked with the sun-god, who is shown holding a wheel, which can symbolise the cycle of life and death.

BELENUS (or Grannus) was the Celtic equivalent of the Roman Apollo, a sun-god who was also responsible for prophecy and the arts, such as music.

EPONA was a horse-goddess. She protected riders and horses, but was also associated with fertility.

CERNUNNOS, 'the horned one', is always shown wearing horns or antlers as lord of the animals. His image is prominent on the Gundestrup Cauldron.

LUG, whose name is still found in such place-names as Lyons, Laon and Leiden, was a warrior, skilled in crafts, and may also have represented fertility. He is identified with the Roman god Mercury.

Of the gods they worship Mercury most of all. He has the greatest number of images; they hold that he is the inventor of all the arts and a guide on the roads and on journeys and they believe him the most influential for money-making and commerce. After him they honour Apollo, Mars, Jupiter and Minerva. Of these deities they have almost the same ideas as other people: Apollo drives away diseases, Minerva teaches the first principles of the arts and crafts, Jupiter rules the heavens and Mars controls the issue of war.

JULIUS CAESAR (100 BC – 44 BC).
Emperor of Rome.
Conquered Germanic tribes, the Gauls and Egypt.

This chapter can only give a very brief overview of the Celts in Europe, but detailed sources of information are listed in the bibliography on p131.

2

IRON AGE BRITAIN

Overview

At the time the Hallstatt culture was at its height in Europe, about the seventh century BC, Iron Age influences began reaching Britain. By 450 BC there were Hallstatt settlements on the east coast of Yorkshire. The La Tène Iron Age, which had begun in Europe during the fifth century BC, was well established in Britain by 250 BC. There are many examples in Britain of the distinctive art style and the two-wheeled war chariots of the European La Tène.

The Belgae, or Belgic tribes, refugees from the advancing might of Rome, arrived in Britain from north-west Gaul about 100 BC, and constructed many large forts. They had had close trading links with Britain for generations, and Belgic coinage had been flowing into the country from the late second century BC. The Britons used it as prototypes for their own coinage.

The Celtic-speaking tribes of England, Scotland and Wales, known to the Romans as Britons, were illiterate, and little of their language survives. The study of skeletal remains gives an average height of 1.65m (5'6") for men, and 1.55m (5'2") for women; average life expectancy was around thirty to forty years, and only 8% of the population reached the age of 45. The Iron Age population of Britain has been estimated as possibly two to three million.

It is not known how the Celts arrived in Britain – we will find

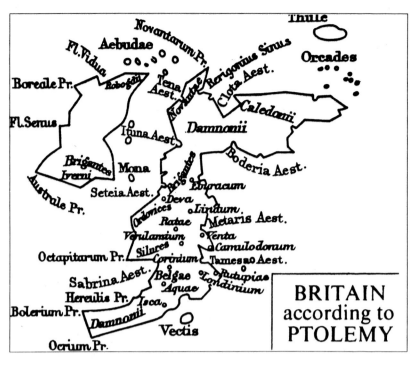

Ireland and Britain according to Ptolemy (2nd century AD). Note that the brigantes are to be found on both sides of the Irish Sea.

The interior of Britain is inhabited by people who claim, on the strength of an oral tradition, to be aboriginal; the coast, by Belgic immigrants who came to plunder and make war – nearly all of them retaining the names of the tribes from which they originated – and later settled down to till the soil. The population is exceedingly large, the ground thickly studded with homesteads, closely resembling those of the Gauls, and the cattle very numerous. For money they use either bronze, or gold coins, or iron ingots of fixed weights. Tin is found inland, and small quantities of iron near the coast; the copper that they use is imported. There is timber of every kind, as in Gaul, except beech and fir. Hares, fowl and geese they think it unlawful to eat, but rear them for pleasure and amusement. The climate is more temperate than that in Gaul, the cold being less severe.

JULIUS CAESAR, *The Conquest of Gaul.*

the same problem when we come to look at Iron Age Ireland. Groups of Celts obviously arrived from the various areas of the European continent, over several hundred years, but whether they came as travellers, immigrants or military conquerors is impossible to say. The development of defensive forts during these centuries might be evidence of a disturbed and unstable period, when people found they had to defend themselves.

Iron Age Britain's cross-channel trade was mainly with northern Gaul. The British Celts imported olive oil and wine, and exported corn, cattle, hides, slaves and hunting dogs, according to Strabo, writing in the first century AD. This long-established trade was part of the reason why Julius Caesar decided to invade Britain in 55 BC. Trying to conquer the Gaulish Celts, he found that the Veneti tribe, in north-western Gaul, had very close links with British tribes, who were probably helping them to fight Rome.

Caesar could not control the channel unless he defeated the Veneti, and once he had done this, he turned his attention to Britain. Here he managed to defeat some tribes, while winning others over to his side. He entered into a treaty of friendship with the Trinovantes, who lived north of the Thames, along the coast. Other tribes we can name from this period are the Cantii of Kent, the Iceni of East Anglia, the Parisi of East Yorkshire and the Brigantes in northern England. Caesar merely established a Roman bridgehead

---

By far the most civilised inhabitants are those living in Kent (a purely maritime district), whose way of life differs little from that of the Gauls. Most of the tribes in the interior do not grow corn but live on milk and meat, and wear skins. All the Britons dye their bodies with woad, which produces a blue colour, and this gives them a more terrifying appearance in battle. They wear their hair long, and shave the whole of their bodies except the head and the upper lip. Wives are shared between groups of ten or twelve men, especially between brothers and between fathers and sons; but the offspring of these unions are counted as the children of the man with whom a particular woman cohabited first.

JULIUS CAESAR, *The Conquest of Gaul.*

in Britain; the subsequent Roman conquest was carried out by the Emperor Claudius, from 43 BC on.

England

Iron was first worked in England from about the seventh century BC, using the plentiful deposits of iron ores. We do not know how or by whom the knowledge of iron-smelting was introduced. A typical iron-producing site is Brooklands, in Surrey, where iron was worked continuously, from the Iron Age, up to a hundred years ago. The Iron Age blacksmith used the same array of tongs, hammers, anvils and chisels as blacksmiths of any age, and some of them travelled around the country, carrying their equipment with them. There seems to have been an aura of magic about the blacksmith's craft, and the skills were kept shrouded in mystery.

A notable aspect of continental Iron Age culture is the construction of hillforts, and Britain has over 3,000. Many of them are very small, homesteads rather than defensive forts. The greatest concentration of large hillforts runs along the south coast of England, and includes such impressive sites as Danebury in Hampshire, dating to the sixth and fifth centuries BC.

There seems to have been a social change in the fourth century BC. This may mean that the first La Tène influences were reaching the country, although it was about a hundred years before the La Tène Iron Age was fully established in Britain. This change saw some hillforts becoming much larger, apparently dominating others and acting as political centres. These are called 'developed hillforts', and examples include Uffington Castle, in Oxfordshire, and a later stage of Maiden Castle, in Dorset. They were not just military forts; family groups also lived in them.

In a short book like this, it is best just to mention a couple of sites which are important for the English Iron Age – a complete overview would be impossible. The site of Gussage All Saints, in Dorset, was an enclosed settlement occupied from about 500 BC to the end of the first century AD, containing numerous round houses.

Above: *Snettisham gold torque. Diameter 199mm. Photograph courtesy British Museum.*
Below: *Waltham Abbey Hoard. Blacksmith's tools – tongs, anvil, head of sledgehammer and file. File 232mm long. Photograph courtesy British Museum.*

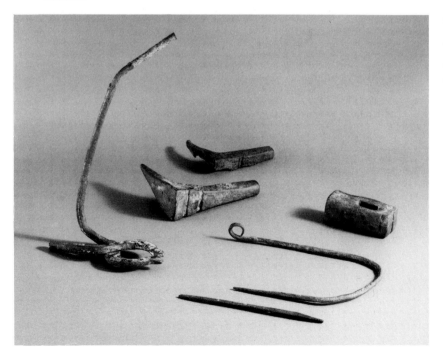

Above: *Wandsworth bronze round boss. Photograph courtesy British Museum.*
Below: *Dunaverney flesh hook. Photograph courtesy British Museum.*

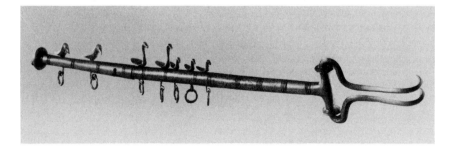

Above: *Deal bronze scabbard with repousée work.*
Photograph courtesy British Museum.

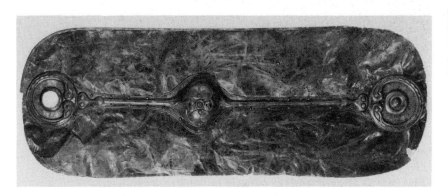

Above: *Witham shield central boss, beaded with coral.*
Length 1.13m. Photograph courtesy British Museum.

A wooden bucket with bronze ornaments found in an Iron Age cemetery in Aylesford, Kent, England. British Museum, London. Height excluding handle mounts 300mm. Photograph AKG London, by Erich Lessing.

A bronze human head on the handle of the wooden bucket (opposite), found in Aylesford, Kent, England. British Museum, London. Photograph AKG London, by Erich Lessing

A self-sufficient community, it produced its own pottery and textiles, grew its own grain, and reared cattle, sheep and goats. Gussage All Saints is notable for the remains of a bronze-working centre, and large numbers of broken moulds and crucibles were found. The technology shown is very advanced, and the community must have been wealthy enough to support a number of smiths while they worked. The smiths may have lived there permanently, or called by at intervals. The bronze worked was almost all in the form of horse-bridles and chariot fittings, and it was obviously a specialist manufacturing centre.

We tend to think of Iron Age wooden houses as being cramped and squalid huts, but modern experiment, based on excavation evidence, has created a replica Iron Age house at Pimperne Down in Dorset. This fine building, with an inner and an outer wall, is over 13 m. in diameter and needed more than 200 trees for its construction; the roof is thatched. In engineering terms, it was more complex to construct than a block-built stone temple, and must have needed large numbers of skilled technicians, as well as access to suitable timber, managed and grown for the purpose. This was obviously a prestigious house; simpler houses are also known, with walls made of stakes interwoven with hazel or willow rods and plastered with clay ('wattle and daub' construction), standing about 1.50 m. high.

A large barrow-cemetery at Arras, in East Yorkshire, gave its name to the Arras Culture, which is dated around the third century BC (La Tène Iron Age). About a dozen cart-burials were found here, each containing a two-wheeled cart, and a distinctive shape of small square 'barrow' or burial mound was used; thousands of these barrows have now been identified in East Yorkshire. There are few grave goods, mainly brooches and crude pottery.

The biggest Yorkshire cemetery, at Wetwang Slack, contains 486 barrows. Here, two cart-burials produced two swords in decorated scabbards, each accompanying a male body; an adjoining grave, of a young woman, contained a sealed bronze canister (called the 'bean-tin' by the excavators) which is covered with very similar

*Reconstruction of the burial of a Celtic chieftain at
Wetwang Slack, Yorkshire. Painting by Peter Connolly.*

decoration. This may have been a family group. A grave in Kirkburn, the next parish, contained a sword with the finest decorated hilt known from Celtic Britain.

Druids accompanied the Celts to Britain, and there are many remains of religious shrines, statues and sacred places. The Celtic cult of the head became widespread. Ritual and sacrifice were extremely important, and Caesar says that the worst punishment a druid could impose was to ban someone from worship. Wetland sites such as lakes were the focus of much of the ritual, but groves of trees could also have sacred significance.

Representations of all the well-known Celtic gods are found in Britain, particularly a warrior-god who is equated with Mars, but there were also various local British cults. The cult of Nodens, a warrior but also a god of healing, is one of the best-known, and an impressive stone-built temple to him survives at Lydney Park, overlooking the Severn Estuary. Stone temples were not built in Britain until the Romans came, when a kind of Romano-Celtic religion developed. By this time the druids had been exterminated.

The greater part of the island is level and under timber, but it contains many hilly districts. It produces corn, cattle, gold, silver, and iron. All these are exported, and also hides, slaves, and powerfully built dogs for the chase. The men are of higher stature than the Gauls, and less fair-haired, but their flesh is more puffy. Here is proof of their size. We ourselves saw in Rome British striplings who overtopped the tallest men there by a clear half-foot; but they were bandy-legged and badly proportioned in all their limbs. Their customs resemble those of the Gauls, but are more simple and primitive. Some of them have plenty of milk, but cannot make it into cheese for lack of knowledge; they are likewise ignorant of garden cultivation and other husbandry. They are governed by hereditary kings; in war they mostly rely on chariots, like some of the Gauls. Their strongholds are forest enclosures: they fence off a wide ring with hewn timber and build huts for themselves, and stalls for their cattle, for a short season. Their climate is rainy rather than snowy. In the open air the mist holds on for long, so that in the course of a whole day the sun will only be visible for a few noontide hours.

STRABO

Scotland

The late Bronze Age in Scotland saw contacts with the Hallstatt cultures of Europe, apparently before the rest of Britain, but by the first and second century AD, Scotland's culture was closely related to the La Tène Iron Age in England. Scotland was never conquered by the Romans, who instead constructed Hadrian's Wall to keep out such tribes as the Maeatae and the Caledonii. Some placenames and tribal names indicate clear connections between Scotland and south Britain. For example, the Damnonii of south-western Scotland must relate to the Dumnonii in south-western England, and the Cornavii of Caithness must be connected with the Cornavii of North Wales. The Britons inhabited Scotland until the fifth century AD, when an invasion from Ireland changed the political scene.

Roos Carr group of figures on a boat-base with animal head. Photograph, Hull and East Riding Museum, Kingston upon Hull City Museums, Galleries and Archives, England.

The Scottish Iron Age is divided into three cultural stages:

1. South of the line of the Clyde and Forth, there is a certain amount of bronze metalwork in La Tène style, such as scabbards and cloak-pins. It is possible this style was brought by La Tène Celts moving up from Yorkshire. Other indicators of Iron Age culture include rotary querns (a technologically-advanced type of corn-grinder), and translucent glass armlets.

Mousa Broch, Shetland – tower fortress typical of Scotland in this period. Photograph Dennis Coutts, Lerwick, Shetland Islands.

2. East of the central massif of Scotland, the evidence of Iron Age activity is quite sparse. The most important distinguishing feature of this part of the country is the presence of 'vitrified forts', stone-walled hillforts with timber frames, the oldest probably dating back to the eighth century BC and therefore Bronze Age. Their name comes from the 'vitrification' of their stone walls, which turned into a type of glass as they were burned down. This area seems to have had close links with north Germany in the seventh century BC, but there are no links with the classic La Tène cultures. It was here that the kingdom of the Picts emerged, several centuries later.

3. The Atlantic Province is the name given to the maritime zone west and north of the highland massif, and includes the islands. The Iron Age here is defined by the presence of 'brochs', defensive wooden round-houses surrounded by thick, hollow stone walls. None can be dated earlier than the first century BC, and they seem to have developed locally. This culture is noted for its pottery styles, but no decorated metalwork of any kind has been found. The rotary quern used is a type called a 'disc quern', from its distinctive thin profile. This Atlantic culture may have resulted from new incursions from the continent, tribes moving ahead of the Romans, in the first century BC.

Wales

The late Bronze Age in Wales showed a distinct move to fortified settlements, indicating a warlike or disturbed situation. By the early Iron Age, hillforts were widespread in the eastern part of Wales. The most common form of occupation site, of course, was the small individual farmstead. These were mostly built in timber, but later they were also constructed of stone – possibly timber reserves were being used up.

The knowledge of ironworking probably came to Wales from south-west England, but its use only became widespread in the first century BC. There is evidence for the use of Welsh iron ore, particularly in the north-west; it must have been widely traded, as finds of Gaulish coins make clear. Salt was also produced and traded. Pottery is rare. The Welsh Celts were obviously in the mainstream of trade, having maritime links with the continent and the rest of Britain.

By the late second century AD, the Romans record Wales as being divided into at least four tribal areas, the Ordovices, the Deceangli, the Demetae and the Silures.

Few Welsh Iron Age burials have survived. There were some ritual deposits of valuable goods in wetland areas such as Llyn Cerrig Bach, now a bog but probably once a lake. The dates of the deposits at this site run from the second century BC to the first century AD. Celtic Wales is noteworthy as the site of the last stand of the druids, in Anglesey. The continental druids had been gradually driven west by Caesar, who understood all too well their role in uniting the Celtic tribes against him. The survivors finally reached Anglesey, and it was here that they were exterminated by Roman forces.

Art

Notable examples of British La Tène art are the Ratcliffe shield-boss, found in the Trent river, and two scabbards found in

Back of a mirror from Desborough, Northamptonshire, England. Engraved bronze (6th – 1st BC). Size 26cm. British Museum, London. Photograph AKG London, by Erich Lessing.

the river Thames. From this time on, British art began to move away from its continental influences, and developed what is called by Ian Stead 'Stage IV'. Masterpieces of this stage include a shield and scabbard from the River Witham, and two shield-bosses found in the Thames at Wandsworth. Some of the designs, given the name 'Scabbard Style', are closely related to those on scabbards found in Ireland, in the Bann river and nearby.

This was followed by Stead's Stage V, which used to be called the 'Mirror Style', and is dated to the second and first centuries BC. It is completely insular in inspiration, and is found on a number of beautifully-decorated bronze mirrors, which cannot be matched on the continent at all. The mirrors are found in two groups, one situated between Devon and Northamptonshire, and one in the south-east, between Buckinghamshire and Essex. Other examples of this style are found on artefacts from the bogland site of Llyn Cerrig Bach, in Wales. With its curvilinear and triskele (three-fold) patterns, it exemplifies the highest skills of late Iron Age artists and metalworkers. But it marked the end of individual British development; already the Romans were drawing near.

Other decorative metalworking is found on the fibulae, bronze safety-pin-type brooches, which were widespread throughout the British Isles in the Iron Age. These brooches were known on the continent, but distinctive insular British styles developed. Pins and bracelets were also worn, but few survive. There was also, of course, the Celtic torque. A site in Snettisham, Norfolk, has produced five hoards of Iron Age gold and silver, which include seventy-five torques. This 'Gold Field' must have contained the wealth of a whole community of Britons. One of the torques, the 'Great Torque', is said to be one of England's finest antiquities.

In chariot fighting the Britons begin by driving all over the field hurling javelins, and generally the terror inspired by the horses and the noise of the wheels are sufficient to throw their opponents' ranks into disorder. Then, after making their way between the squadrons of their own cavalry, they jump down from the chariots and engage on foot. In the meantime their charioteers retire a short distance from the battle and place the chariots in such a position that their masters, if hard pressed by numbers, have an easy means of retreat to their own lines. Thus they combine the mobility of cavalry with the staying-power of infantry; and by daily training and practice they attain such proficiency that even on a steep incline they are able to control the horses at full gallop, and to check and turn them in a moment. They can run along the chariot pole, stand on the yoke, and get back into the chariot as quick as lightning.

JULIUS CAESAR, *The Conquest of Gaul*

3

IRON AGE IRELAND

The Pre-Celtic Bronze Age

Between the eighth and sixth centuries BC, while the Hallstatt Iron Age was developing in Europe, Ireland was continuing its Bronze Age. Bronze Age Ireland was a wealthy country, producing beautiful artefacts of gold and amber, with trading contacts in Britain and other parts of western Europe. The economic system was based on ploughing and stock-rearing; cattle were an important source of wealth. Few burials can be dated to this period, because cremation was the preferred burial method, with the ashes interred in pits, and traces of them are hard to find.

The population increased rapidly, living in family groups in small dwellings. Most of these groups were no larger than a small village. However, some larger defended sites are also known, such as the *crannóg*, which was a type of fenced homestead built on brushwood platforms over or near water. There were also some hillforts, large defended sites on hilltops. It was once assumed that the construction of hillforts was associated only with the Iron Age, and had been brought to Ireland by the Celts, but excavations at Rathgall, Co. Wicklow and Haughey's Fort, Co. Armagh have dated these two hillforts to the Late Bronze Age. The dates of other hillforts are also being pushed back.

An explosion of metal-working is associated with the pre-Celtic

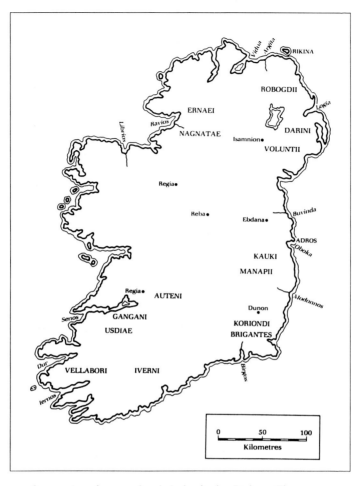

One version of a map of early Ireland, after Ptolemy. The locations are mostly speculative.

Ireland is a large island, of greater length than breadth, extending along the north side of Britain. We have nothing definite to say about it, save that its inhabitants are wilder than the Britons, being cannibals and coarse feeders, and think it decent to eat up their dead parents and to have open intercourse with women, even with mothers and sisters. But for these statements we have no trustworthy authority.

STRABO

[Britain] is triangular, with one side facing Gaul. One corner of this side, on the coast of Kent, is the landing-place for nearly all the ships from Gaul, and point east; the lower corner points south. The length of this side is about 475 miles. Another side faces west, towards Spain. In this direction is Ireland, which is supposed to be half the size of Britain, and lies at the same distance from it as Gaul. Midway across is the Isle of Man, and it is believed that there are also a number of smaller islands, in which according to some writers there is a month of perpetual darkness at the winter solstice.

JULIUS CAESAR, *The Conquest of Gaul*

Bronze Age, which produced not only the beautiful gold jewellery which ranks with the best of any such work in the ancient world, but a mass of warlike equipment – swords, spears and shields.

Combined with the development of defended sites at about the same time, this implies a period of conflict between tribal groups. The development of trade and such industries as metalworking needs a fairly secure political system, and the ruling dynasties which provided this stability would also have been rivals for land and power.

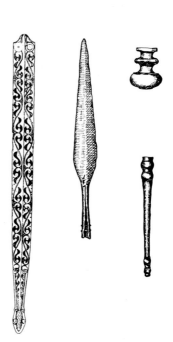

Lisnacrogher scabbard and other small items of metalwork. Courtesy Professor Barry Raftery.

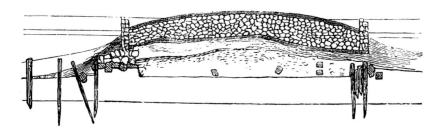

Above: *(top) Crannóg hut, reconstructed at Craggaunowen, Co Clare.*
Photograph Brian Lynch. Courtesy Bord Failte – The Irish Tourist Board..
(bottom) Section through the Ardakillen crannóg, Co. Roscommon, showing how
the crannógs were built up. After Wood-Martin, Pagan Ireland.

Opposite: *Reconstruction of a La Tène house of the 1st BC from Roggendorf,*
Lower Austria. Kitchen corner: fireplace, kettle, utensils, farm tools, on the right
a quern. Museum für Vorgeschichte, Aspam/Zaya, Austria. Photograph AKG
London, by Erich Lessing.

Early Iron Age

The Hallstatt Iron Age was established in Europe from the eighth century BC, and iron-smelting was being practised in Britain by the mid-seventh century BC. Iron-working was introduced to Ireland around the same time. Almost fifty Hallstatt C type swords have been found, mostly in rivers and in the northern part of the island. They were made in bronze, but are closely related in size and shape to iron sword-types from Britain. The existence of these swords does not necessarily mean invasion; this type of sword was fashionable all over western Europe, and Ireland was simply part of the wide area in which developments in style and technology were easily exchanged. Gold-working, which had reached such a pitch of perfection, seems to stop altogether at this time; the indigenous gold may have been worked out.

We have some iron finds of Irish manufacture from these centuries. They include socketed axe-heads, and a cauldron of riveted iron sheets found in Co. Cavan. To add to this meagre evidence of possible early Celtic influence, two excavated settlement sites, one in Aughinish, Co. Limerick, and a crannóg in Rathtinaun, Co. Sligo, have produced iron artefacts. The iron objects that survive from this early period seem to cluster around the Shannon river and the Bann river, two entry routes which led to easily-accessible iron ore deposits. They could mark the movement of travelling blacksmiths, or small groups of immigrants with such skills; there is no evidence of any more powerful influence.

But that's all there is of the early Iron Age in Ireland. Knowledge of iron-working technology reached the country, and then seems to have died away without developing further. The next signs of iron-working can be dated four hundred years later, about the third century BC, when the La Tène culture reached Ireland; it had already passed its peak in Europe, but was still vibrant in Britain. This is the beginning of Ireland's Iron Age proper, and the first real signs of Celtic influence. The centuries between are a kind of

Iron cauldron from Drumlane, Co. Cavan.
Photograph National Museum of Ireland.

archaeological Dark Age, when the country went into an economic decline. Very few finds can be reliably dated to this period.

Various reasons are put forward for the decline. Climatic conditions were worsening, producing increased cold and heavy rain. Sea levels were fluctuating, leading to coastal erosion. The growing population and the wider forest clearances of the Bronze Age had put more pressure on fertile land, exhausting it. Agriculture had been practised in Ireland for almost three thousand years, but in the Bronze Age the newly-introduced *ard*, a type of plough, meant that soil was disturbed more deeply than it had been by simple spades and digging-sticks.

Gradually nutrients were lost from the disturbed layers, because of the amount of rain leaching the soil; fertilisation was inadequate. The growing population meant that there was less and less unused land available, and fields had less time to recover between crops. Bogs began to spread more rapidly. As land became scarcer and more valuable, the struggle to possess it would become more violent, and this could account for the large numbers of weapons which survive.

The late Bronze Age was notable for the deposition of over 150

Warriors with lurs (Celtic wind instruments). Gundestrup Cauldron, inner plate. Embossed silver, gilded (1st BC). National Museum, Copenhagen, Denmark. Photograph AKG London, by Erich Lessing.

large hoards of gold and bronze objects – 'offerings' to the gods, deposited in rivers and lakes, or buried in fields. These may represent desperate attempts to delay or turn aside bad fortune, as the weather got colder and wetter, and possibly also fear of political and military upheaval of some kind. In what seem to have been extremely precarious economic conditions, it is no wonder a new technology could not make much headway.

Celtic head, possibly a god, Armagh Cathedral, Northern Ireland.
Photograph by Robert Vance. Courtesy of Don Sutton Photo Library.

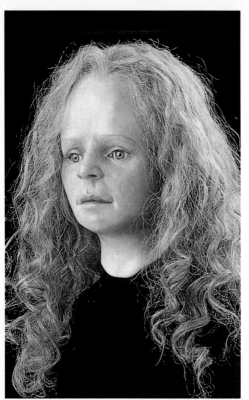

Left: *Head of 'Yde Girl'. Reconstructed from the 'bog body' of a young girl, found in Holland. Photograph J. Bosma. Courtesy of Provincial Museum of Drenthe, Holland.*

Below: *Gold and amber jewellery found in the tomb of a princess. Discovered in 1954 in Reinheim, Germany. Museum für Vor-und Frühgeschichte, Saarbrücken, Germany. Photograph AKG London, by Erich Lessing.*

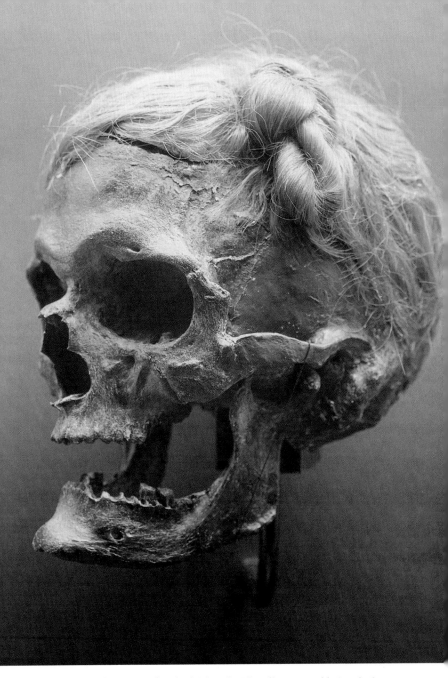

Skull of Osterby Man, a 'bog body' found with well-preserved hairstyle, known as a 'Swabian knot'. Photograph courtesy of the Archäologisches Landesmuseum, Schleswig.

Above: *Bronze sword hilt, Ballyshannon Bay, Co. Donegal. National Museum of Ireland.*

Right: *Embossed bronze shield inlaid with red enamel, a classic example of British La Tène art (6th – 1st BC), found in the Thames at Battersea, London. Height 85cm.*
British Museum, London.
Photograph AKG London, by Erich Lessing.

Opposite (top): *The Grianan of Aileach, Co. Donegal, seven miles south of Fahan, one of the great stone fortresses in Ireland in use in Celtic times. (Partially restored.) Photograph by Robert Vance. Courtesy of Don Sutton Photo Library.*

Opposite (bottom): *Reconstructed crannóg (lake dwelling) at Ferrycarrig National Heritage Park, Co. Wexford. Photograph Brian Lynch. Courtesy of Bord Fáilte.*

Above: *The god Cernunnos, Lord of the Wild Beasts, amidst animals, holding a snake and a torque. From the Gundestrup Cauldron, inner plate. Embossed silver (1st BC). National Museum, Copenhagen, Denmark. Photograph AKG London, by Erich Lessing.*

Left: *Gold model of a Celtic sea-going boat, from the Broighter hoard. National Museum of Ireland.*

A Celtic hero. Stone head (2nd – 1st BC) found at Mšecké Žehrovice. Size 25cm. National Museum, Prague. Photograph AKG London, by Erich Lessing.

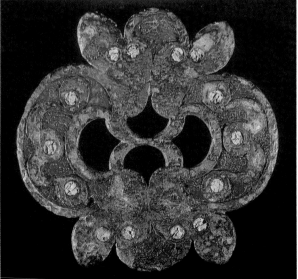

Above: *Iron Age Tollund Man as he was found, with a ligature round his neck. Photograph from Silkeborg Museum, Denmark.*

Left: *Openwork bronze plaque from a horse harness with red and yellow enamel (1st BC). Found in London. Height 8.5cm. British Museum, London. Photograph AKG London, by Erich Lessing.*

Loughnashade trumpet. Photograph National Museum of Ireland.

La Tène Iron Age

It would be convenient to be able to date the Celtic arrival in Ireland in relation to known events in Europe or in Britain, but we cannot. We do not know which particular tribe of Celts brought the La Tène Iron Age to Ireland, or how many of them, nor do we have any date for arrival more specific than around the third century BC. They could have come from any part of Europe – France, Britain, Spain. Many aspects of Ireland's La Tène culture are very different from the European La Tène, which was already being threatened by Rome by the time it reached Ireland. It lasted in this island outpost long after it had been superseded elsewhere.

There is not one chariot burial known in Ireland, nor do we have any Iron Age pottery, and there are no huge cemeteries like those found elsewhere in Europe. Indeed, hardly any definitely Iron Age burials can be identified in Ireland, which could be an argument against the theory of an invasion by a completely new culture which overwhelmed the old. The Bronze Age tradition of cremation, in pits or sometimes under ring-barrows, obviously remained dominant. The main ethnic element of the so-called Celtic Iron Age population in Ireland was rooted in the indigenous Bronze Age population.

Only a limited number of European La Tène characteristics are found in Ireland, and they are mostly on objects of Irish manufacture. La Tène carvings are found on stone monuments, showing that the art style was not just imported, it was practised here. The style could have been transmitted through trading contacts, and iron-using craftsmen emigrating to Ireland might pass on their skills to the indigenous bronze-smiths, who were already highly skilled in metalworking. The earliest La Tène material of Irish manufacture can be dated to 300 – 200 BC, but there seems to have been a second wave of material, probably from British immigrants, about 100 BC. Of the very few Iron Age burials we can be sure of, none is earlier than the first century BC.

By about 100 AD, some Roman material can be found in Ireland, particularly in Leinster. Whether the Romans ever reached Ireland in any numbers is a matter of controversy, but there must have been trading contacts with Roman Britain. By the fourth century AD, Iron Age material was being completely replaced by Late Roman types, and the coming of Christianity in the fifth century AD completed this process.

The most notable aspect of the La Tène material in Ireland is that it is concentrated completely in the northern half of the country. None is known from Munster or south Leinster, yet there must have been a Late Iron Age of some sort in these areas as well. The large hillforts, which were once supposed to indicate a Celtic Iron Age presence, are concentrated in the south, not the La Tène north, but we do not yet know enough about who built them and why. Some of the most recent excavation is pushing their dates back to the Bronze Age.

The La Tène art which is found on such articles as ornate horse-trappings obviously belonged to an élite class, and we know very little about the ordinary population – Barry Raftery refers to them as 'the invisible people'. Certainly some elements of the culture are completely new to Ireland, such as a new type of quern,

Stone head, approximately 25 cm high, Camlyball, Armagh. Photograph Ulster Museum.

the beehive quern, and the developed ironworking technology, but they need not have come about through population movements. They could just as easily be spread through trade, immigration, or Irish emigrants coming home from abroad.

However, when it comes to deciding whether Celts came to Ireland, or when, the most important piece of evidence is provided by the Irish language. Old Irish, which was the language the Christian missionaries found when they arrived, is unquestionably a Celtic language, however many influences it had absorbed over the centuries. And language can *only* be spread by groups of settlers, not by trade or isolated travellers.

Modern Celtic languages are divided into 'P-Celtic' and 'Q-Celtic' forms, distinguished by differences in spelling and pronunciation. While the Celtic language over most of Europe developed into P-Celtic (sometimes called 'Brythonic'), Ireland preserved the earlier Q-Celtic language (or 'Goidelic') which ultimately became Old Irish. Q-Celtic dialects were also dominant in Spain, at one time. The only other surviving Q-Celtic languages are Manx, and Scots Gaelic. This came from Ireland to Scotland in the fifth century AD, when the Irish invaded, but up till then the Britons of Scotland had used a P-Celtic dialect.

Welsh, Cornish and Breton are all P-Celtic. As a simple illustration, the Old Welsh word for 'son', *map*, is the P-Celtic form of the Irish word for 'son', *mac*. We don't know when the change from Q to P occurred in Europe, but it had happened by 325 BC. This may mean that the language in Ireland had lost contact with other Celtic languages before this time, and stayed in the older form.

Effects of iron

In Europe, the coming of iron brought with it major social and economic changes. It was a cheaper technology than bronze, and the material was more readily available. Large quantities of goods, such as pots and knives, could be provided for even the least important social groups. Its development in Ireland must have brought about much the same degree of change, although iron ore was not so widely available. We know very little about how iron was manufactured in Ireland, but many of the techniques were developments of sophisticated bronze-working methods, such as riveting and punching, and the use of sheet metal.

Only a handful of sites have produced remains of smelting and forging, but this is more likely to have been due to a shortage of smiths, rather than of materials. We have not found any large centres of iron production, such as are found all over the continent. The Irish smiths were at least as competent as those in Britain and Europe, producing prestige pieces as well as household articles and tools.

The earliest Iron Age objects were in fact made in bronze, copying iron types, but by the first century BC almost all tools and weapons were of iron.

> Above Britain lies Iuverna, of nearly equal extent, but of oblong shape, with two sides of the same length. Its climate is unfavourable for the maturing of crops, but there is such a profuse growth of grass, and this is as sweet as it is rich, that the cattle can sate themselves in a short part of the day, and unless they are kept from continual browsing on the pasture they will burst asunder. The cultivators of the land are uncouth and ignorant of accomplishments beyond all other races, and are utterly lacking in any sense of duty.
>
> POMPONIUS MELA, geographer
> from *De Situ Orbis*, published around AD 40, in Rome.

Ireland in classical writings

Our earliest written evidence about Celtic Ireland comes from the account in the *Geography* of the classical scholar Ptolemy (AD 90 – 168), an Egyptian astronomer and geographer. He divided the known world into twenty-six sections, and the first of these covers Britain and Ireland, using many sources which are now lost.

Many of the fifty-six tribes and places Ptolemy names in relation to Ireland are supposed to be Celtic, but there is little agreement about their interpretation. Some of them may have been derived from similar names which he lists for Britain, and some of them are given in P-Celtic form. The information about Ireland probably came originally from British merchants, in their own language, and then may have passed through several languages before reaching Ptolemy, who used Greek forms. He does seem to provide definite evidence that there were Celtic-speaking people in Ireland at this time.

In soil and climate, in the disposition, temper and habits of its population, it differs but little from Britain. We know most of its harbours and approaches, and that through the intercourse of commerce...I have often heard Agricola [a military leader] say that a single legion with a few auxiliaries could conquer and occupy Ireland.

TACITUS (55-120 AD)
Roman historian, son-in-law of Agricola.

Writers of the present time have nothing to say of anything beyond Ierne, which is just north of Britain. The natives are wholly savage and lead a wretched existence because of the cold. In my opinion it is there that the limits of the habitable earth should be fixed.

STRABO

Ireland and The Romans

Although this book is about the Celts in Ireland, it is necessary to include something about the Romans and their influence, for the sake of completeness. Numerous objects of Roman origin have been found, but not many of them have a proper archaeological context; they could have been brought to Ireland at any time over the succeeding centuries. Of the material that does seem to be dated reliably, some dates to the first and second centuries AD, and some to the fourth and fifth centuries AD – there is nothing from the third century AD. Evidence is mostly found along the coast, from east to north, but some items were found further south.

There is a good deal of argument about whether the Romans actually came to Ireland or not. Most of the finds can be explained as goods brought over by merchants, and others could be booty from Irish raids on the Roman settlements in Britain, which were quite

The Roman fort at Drumangh, Co. Meath, graphic by Roy Cooper and Jenny Preece. Courtesy Sunday Times.

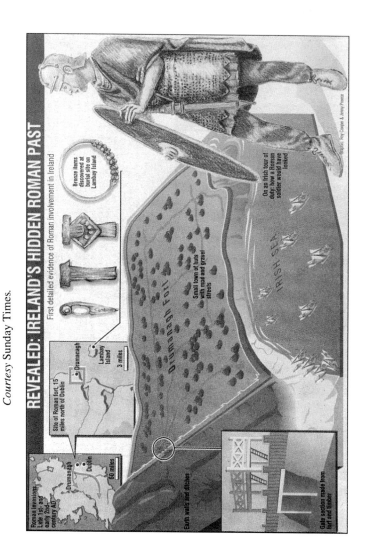

REVEALED: IRELAND'S HIDDEN ROMAN PAST

First detailed evidence of Roman involvement in Ireland

Roman invasions Late 1st- and early 2nd-century AD

Drumanagh

Dublin

60 miles

Site of Roman fort, 15 miles north of Dublin

Drumanagh

Lambay Island

3 miles

Bronze items discovered at burial site on Lambay Island

Drumanagh Fort

Small town of huts with mud and gravel streets

IRISH SEA

On an Irish tour of duty how a Roman soldier would have looked

Earth walls and ditches

Gate section made from turf and timber

Graphic: Roy Cooper & Jenny Preece

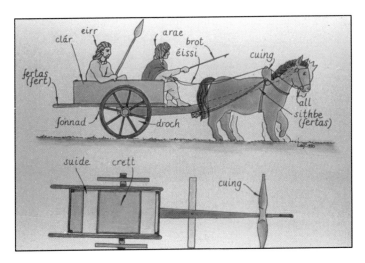

Reconstruction of Irish-style cart. Courtesy of Liam de Paor.

common by the fourth and fifth centuries AD. Irish raiders may have been 'bought off' by being given tribute. It is also possible that Irish fighters served abroad as Roman mercenaries, and were paid in Roman silver and coins.

Interestingly, the Neolithic passage tomb of Newgrange, in the Boyne Valley, was a centre of pilgrimage and a tourist attraction for Roman visitors. At least twenty-five Roman coins have been found deposited there, as well as a small hoard of gold jewellery, possibly as offerings to the Daghdha, 'the father of all', a god with whom the site was associated. Newgrange was apparently also associated with Manannan Mac Lir, a god of the sea. Buried at Newgrange was part of a gold torque, of the middle Bronze Age, which had obviously been cut up for melting and reuse. Roman letters were punched into it, but their meaning is unclear. It must have been dug up in Ireland, but later come into the possession of a Roman.

Some hoards of Roman silver have been found; a hoard at Ballinrees, Co. Derry, contained over 1500 coins, and 200 ounces of plate silver and ingots. The area where the Broighter Hoard was found, around the Roe valley in Co. Derry, also produced a cluster of Roman finds, including a statuette of Mercury. Inscribed silver ingots have been found at Balline, Co. Limerick.

Stonyford, Co. Kilkenny, produced the Roman grave of a woman; the cremated remains were placed in a glass urn, covered with a bronze mirror. This burial, near Waterford harbour, may be evidence of a small permanent Roman settlement, perhaps a trading post. Some signs of a Roman or north British settlement were found at Lambay Island, Co. Dublin. Here several graves were discovered in 1927, but were destroyed before they could be properly examined. Some of the grave goods have survived, including sword fragments, some pieces of decorated sheet bronze, and a bronze torque.

The most important sign of actual Roman life in Ireland lies buried at Dromanagh, a promontory fort near Loughshinny, overlooking Dublin Bay. Here, over ten years ago, Roman artefacts were uncovered on what seems to have been a Roman coastal fort. Covering over 40 acres, it could have housed up to 5,000 people. The finds include coins from the first and second centuries AD. Unfortunately, however, the site is the subject of legal controversy, and cannot be touched until the problems have been resolved. Meanwhile, the existing finds lie hidden and unexamined in the National Museum, Dublin. It is to be hoped that this situation will not drag on for much longer, because it is obvious that this site could transform our ideas about Romans in Ireland.

None of these signs of Roman influence yet add up to any kind of invasion, or even a military presence. Ireland may have had fewer European contacts after the Roman invasion of Britain. But certainly links with Britain remained close, and went in both directions. After all, the coming of St Patrick to Ireland in the fifth century AD was ultimately due to his kidnapping, in earlier years, by Irish raiders who attacked Roman British settlements to capture slaves.

4

PHYSICAL REMAINS

Human Remains

Very few individual burials can be dated to the Celtic Iron Age. Only about twenty have been found on sites that are definitely Iron Age, and some others were inserted into earlier, Bronze Age burial mounds, possibly because of some emergency, or a hasty tidying-up after a battle. The burial rite continued to be cremation, under circular barrows. However, the custom of inhumation, that is burying the body unburned and intact (either crouched or lying straight), spread into Ireland from the first century AD. Both types of burial continued to be used side by side, and burial sites enclosed by circular ditches remained the custom.

Iron Age females averaged under 1.50 m. in height, and males 1.70 m. or less. Life expectancy was low; of the Iron Age remains we can study, the average time of death was between twenty and thirty years of age, and very few reached what we would call middle age. A great number of the surviving burials are of children, sometimes buried in the same graves as adults. The adult skeletons show signs of arthritis, and the teeth are not decayed, though very worn-down. The evidence indicates a well-balanced diet. Some burials are obviously those of immigrants, mainly from Roman Britain, as discussed in the last chapter.

Tollund Man, found in a Danish bog in 1950, preserved with the cap removed to show his closely cropped hair, possibly a mark of punishment. He had been strangled and his throat was cut. Silkeborg Museum, Denmark.

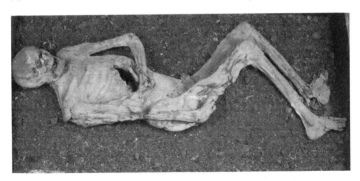

Above: *Gallagh Man, Co. Galway. National Museum of Ireland.*
Below: *Drawing of the Gallagh body as it was found covered partly by a cloak. After U. Mattenberger.*

Bog Bodies

The occasional discovery of well-preserved bodies in European bogs has always attracted fascinated interest, and many of them have been dated to the Iron Age. Bog bodies are very useful because of the information they can reveal about last meals, hairstyles, traces of disease, or even marks of tattoos – material that is lost through normal burial practices. Recent investigation through old archives and the records of museum collections has come up with a total of eighty-nine bodies, or parts of bodies, which are known from Irish bogs. However, only two or three of these can be dated with any reliability to the Iron Age.

A great number of the finds were listed in the 1830s and 1840s, because this is when the great Ordnance Survey of Ireland was being carried out. People were being interviewed about events, geographical features and placenames in their locality, and any interesting story was recorded. Presumably, some of these accounts of discoveries date back much further than the date they were recorded. In most cases, the remains had been lost or destroyed. The other great period of discovery was in the 1950s, when turf supplies were being exploited because of the post-war lack of coal. The foundation of Bord na Mona in 1948 increased the exploitation of bogs, and probably some remains were lost because of the use of machinery.

One body dated to the Iron Age was found at Gallagh, Co. Galway, in 1821, and is now in the National Museum, Dublin. It was not preserved properly at the time and has decayed to some extent. Descriptions of the finding say it was a young man, with long hair and a beard, covered in a leather or deerskin cape. Around the neck was a band of sally rods, and it was suggested that he had been strangled with these. There was a pointed stake driven into the ground at each side of the body.

Another body of probable Iron Age date, from Baronstown West, Co. Kildare (now lost), consisted of an adult male lying on his back. There were traces of a woollen textile, and parts of a leather garment; he may have been wrapped in a shroud. A late Bronze Age or early Iron Age date can be given to the body of a woman, buried under a bog with the skull of an infant, from Derrymaquirk, Co. Roscommon, but this was a skeleton, not a preserved body. It was accompanied by sheep/goat and dog bones, and the tip of an antler tine.

The whole subject of bog bodies attracts a good deal of argument about the circumstances of the deaths, and the notion of human sacrifice. Certainly, the Celts are supposed to have used human sacrifice, and most of the bog bodies found throughout Europe can be dated to the late Celtic era, during the first century BC and the first century AD. It is also possible that deliberate burial of individuals in such places was connected with the punishment of criminals or people who broke the social laws – outcasts, in other words. It could have been based on superstition, preventing suicides or victims of accidental death from haunting the living. In most circumstances, deliberate burial in a soft bog would be very difficult without the participants sinking in as well. It would have needed a very definite motive.

Many of the bodies do show marks of violence, and undoubtedly some died of their injuries. They could have been the victims of attackers or thieves, who dumped the bodies. Death can result from any number of accidental causes; even in a modern society, with all the resources of the emergency services, people die in snowdrifts or are sucked down into marshes before help can arrive. It has been pointed out that the occasional finds of lengths of rope or textile, even around the neck of the corpse, could be the result of frantic attempts to pull someone out of a boghole, or to retrieve the body. However, many of the European bodies were undoubtedly deliberately hanged or strangled, or killed even more brutally, and were buried in a ceremonial way, covered with branches or wrapped in cloaks.

Hillforts

Recent advances in dating, through archaeology, geology, botany and other scientific methods, have greatly increased what we can learn from physical remains such as hillforts and wooden trackways.

'Hillforts', which are defended sites on hilltops surrounded by large banks and ditches, or sometimes by stone walls, have traditionally been dated to the late Iron Age, and were assumed to have been introduced by the Celts. However, new evidence seems to be pushing them back to the Late Bronze Age. There are also some promontory forts, that is, large sites on promontories or mountain spurs defended by a wall, or by a bank and ditch. We don't know the full number or distribution of these large sites, because aerial photography is revealing new examples every year. The present number of hillforts stands at between sixty and eighty, and there are about 250 promontory forts.

The size of these types of earthwork proves that they were important on a tribal level, rather than as homesteads. Their construction needed large numbers of workers, centrally organised and directed. They may have been used as short-term refuges when danger threatened, and a few may even have developed into small towns. Some of them, however, seem to have been used exclusively on ceremonial occasions.

Hillforts and promontory forts are usually described as having military, defensive uses, and undoubtedly some of them had. However, in many cases the banks and ditches were not massive enough to withstand an assault; they would have been easy to climb, and seem to have been as much symbolic as anything else. Perhaps such sites should be seen as having a specific function for their communities – enclosed places for special occasions.

The concept of enclosing a particular place, to mark it off as special, dates back to at least to the Neolithic (New Stone Age, 4,000 years BC). Periodical assemblies could be held in such a place, where a widely-scattered farming community could come together and exchange news, arrange marriages, buy and sell, celebrate the harvest, and consolidate their sense of themselves as a community. The need for such affirmation may have been intensified by economic problems or threats from outside, such as incoming strangers. The druids of Celtic Gaul are described as holding large regular assemblies for sacred functions such as sacrifices, and legal functions such as judgement on crimes.

Few of the Irish hillfort sites have been excavated as yet. Questions of type and date can only be based on the features which show up on the ground, and these can be misleading. Most of the existing excavation evidence dates these sites to the Late Bronze Age. It is notable that hillforts are concentrated in the south and south-west, where there has been no evidence of La Tène Iron Age

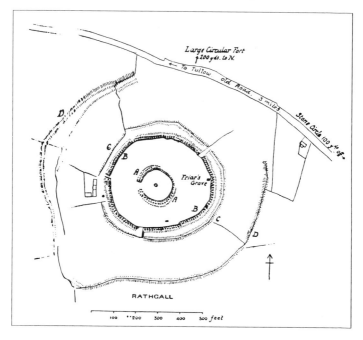

Plan of Rathgall hillfort, Co. Wicklow.

influence at all. Some of them may have been a response by Bronze
Age natives to political instability, or perhaps they were a response
to incomers, who may have been building hillforts too.

Apart from these sites, there is no information about homes or
housing in the Celtic Iron Age. The hundreds of small ringforts
which survive in Ireland belong to the early historic period, or later,
and the small houses found in Navan Fort (see below) are early Iron
Age, or Hallstatt, in date. The 'Rath of the Synods', a circular
enclosed site at Tara, Co. Meath, contains the remains of a small,
oval wooden hut, dated to the first or second centuries AD, but it's
the only definite La Tène period dwelling we have. We can only
surmise that Irish Celtic houses were probably much like the ones
found in Britain.

Site of Emain Macha or Navan Fort, Co. Armagh.
Photograph courtesy Navan at Armagh, The Navan Centre.

Haughey's Fort in Co. Armagh was recently excavated, and produced some evidence of habitation and some pottery, all datable to the late Bronze Age. The hillfort at Rathgall, Co. Wicklow also produced material of the same date, and evidence of bronze-working on the site. Haughey's Fort did produce a couple of dates from the late centuries BC, from radiocarbon dating of charcoal remains, so the site probably had a long life.

Linear Earthworks

Some linear earthworks, lines of bank-and-ditch construction, can be dated to the Iron Age. These include the Black Pig's Dyke, in counties Monaghan and Armagh, which can be said to divide the north from the south, and The Dorsey (meaning 'The Gates') in South Armagh, an irregularly-shaped enclosure which is about 125 hectares in size. These earthworks were being constructed during the last two centuries BC. They could not have been built without the organisation of large numbers of people working together to construct the large banks and ditches. Some of the banks originally had wooden fences along the top.

It has been speculated that these earthworks marked out the barriers of ancient Celtic kingdoms. This might be true, but they contain many gaps, and could not have been defended very well. They may have been designed to regulate movement along major roadways. Certainly they imply that a group of people, large enough to spare workers for this purpose, thought of their earthwork as being a frontier, and also perhaps felt threatened. The earthworks should probably be seen as a way of preventing cattle-raids, rather than a defence against invasion. It is also possible that these discontinuous earthworks were built by different peoples, at different times, and that we are trying to force them into a pattern that is misleading.

However, one important link can be made. When The Dorsey in South Armagh was excavated, the remains of wooden posts found under part of the ramparts could be dated between 400 BC and AD 80. The dating system used is dendrochronology, the counting of tree-rings. The remains of an oak fence produced a felling date of around 95 BC. This is almost exactly the same date as the huge central post of the hillfort at Emain Macha (Navan Fort), also in Co. Armagh. Navan Fort was one of the great so-called 'royal' sites of Iron Age Ireland (see below), and this closeness of date seems to link the centre of ancient Ulster with what may have been its boundary.

The plan of the Corlea Co. Longford, trackway structure.
Courtesy of Professor Barry Raftery.

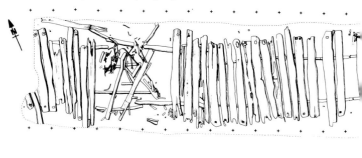

0   1

Trackways

Archaeology in bogs and other wetland sites is making more discoveries every year. Up to the 1980s, there were only seventy recorded accounts of wooden trackways being investigated, and most of these were assumed to be mediaeval, but the number of prehistoric finds has since increased greatly. One of the most important is a wooden trackway discovered under the bog in Corlea, Co. Longford (now open to the public).

The timber in this trackway can be dated by dendrochronology to 148 BC. The oak planks, up to 4 metres in length, were laid transversely on parallel pairs of runners, and secured by wooden pegs. Thousands of timbers were needed, and these had to be transported from several kilometres away. The excavators found that it took six men to carry some of the planks.

The roadway runs for two kilometres, and would have been built for use by carts and wagons. However, it showed no real signs of such use, and seems to have been abandoned for some reason before it was finished. Like the hillforts, it was constructed by a large number of people working to an organised plan. No known settlements in the area can be definitely linked with it, and very few Iron Age objects have been found in the district. It could have led to Cruachain, in Co. Roscommon, which is 35 km away, and was one of the so-called 'royal' sites. Another site named in the ancient texts, Uisneach, lies to the south-east.

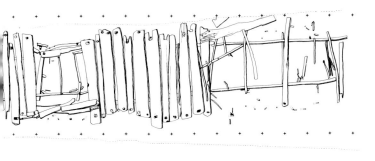

3   4   5M.

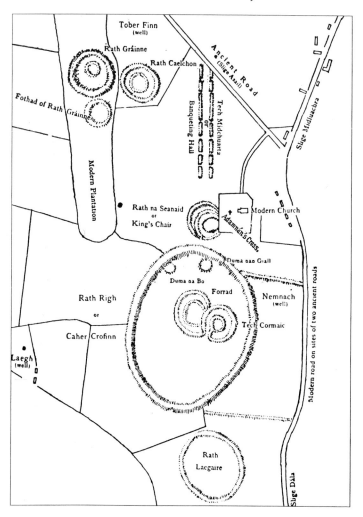

Plan of Tara. From A Social History of Ancient Ireland, *P.W. Joyce. From the two plans given by Petrie in his Essay on Tara.*

*Hill of Tara, legendary religious and cultural centre of ancient Ireland.
Photograph Robert Vance. Courtesy of Don Sutton Photo Library.*

'Royal' Sites

Old and medieval Irish texts refer to 'royal sites', seats of kingship. The best-known 'royal' site in Ireland is, of course, Tara, Co. Meath, referred to in late written sources as the seat of the high-kingship of Ireland. The high-kingship itself was a very late development, within the historic period, but it was back-dated into prehistory by later pseudo-historians to give it the authority of age.

Tara, which is supposed to have been where kings were inaugurated, certainly seems to have been a pre-Christian site of ritual importance. It consists of a complex of earthworks running for almost 900 metres along a commanding ridge. The bulk of the remains belong to the Celtic Iron Age, but at least one monument, a Neolithic passage tomb, dates back 2,500 years earlier, and finds of Roman pottery and glass show that the area was still being used in the first three centuries AD.

Another 'royal' site, Dún Ailinne in County Kildare, is identified in medieval texts as the royal site of Leinster, and is the largest prehistoric site in the province. An 8-metre wide roadway leads through the entrance of the oval bank and ditch, which were not large enough to be defensive. Some evidence of Neolithic habitation was revealed by excavation, but most of the building took place during the Iron Age, not earlier than the third or second centuries BC, and continuing till the second or third century AD.

The excavators found the remains of several circular timber fences or walls, each one built on the remains of the last. The structures may have supported tiered platforms which had a ritual or ceremonial use; there was very little evidence of domestic living. Over 18,000 animal bones were found, more than half of them from cattle and most of the rest from pigs. These animals were probably not raised on the site, but they were certainly eaten there, presumably during festivals of some kind.

Near Baltinglass Hill, in Co. Wicklow, is a series of stone enclosures at a site called Spinans Hill. Aerial photographs revealed a series of ramparts, and showed that a nearby hillfort, Brusselstown

Above: *Dún Ailinne from the air.*
Photograph Department of Arts, Culture and the Gaeltacht.

Below: *Reconstruction of a sanctuary of Dún Ailinne,*
Kildare, 3rd – 2nd century BC .

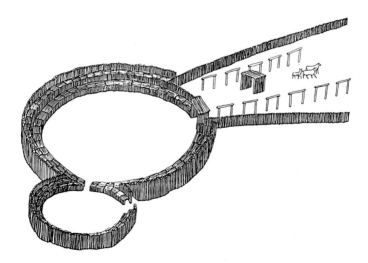

Dún Aengus on Inishmore, Aran Islands, from the air (looking northwest).
Photograph J. K. St Joseph, Cambridge University.

Ring, had two walls instead of the one previously known. A continuous stone-built rampart ran from Brusselstown Ring to enclose almost all of Spinans Hill, forming a huge enclosure of 132 hectares in extent. The date of the site is still unknown. It must have been extremely important at one time, and again required the commitment of large numbers of people to build it.

The Aran Islands, in Co. Galway, contain the spectacular fort of Dún Aengus, on a vertical cliff-edge 100 metres above the sea. There are three massive stone walls, and the remains of a fourth, but what we can see now was heavily restored in the nineteenth century. The most interesting feature of Dún Aengus is its defensive *chevaux-de-frise*. This is a concentration of closely-packed stone spikes, which cover the approach to the fort; they stand about one

The chevaux-de-frise *at Dún Aengus, which defend the approaches from the island side. Photograph Bord Fáilte – Irish Tourist Board.*

metre in height, and are wedged into the limestone bedrock. It is clear that the fort needed to be strongly defended, and therefore it is unlikely that it was used only for ceremonial occasions. Excavation has produced a number of Late Bronze Age finds, such as bone pins, clay moulds for swords and spears, and a bronze chisel. Signs of settlement were found over the whole area, but there was little evidence of Iron Age occupation.

The *chevaux-de-frise* idea, found in three other Irish forts which are all in the west of the country, is widely known in Iron Age Spain, and is also found in Britain and France. It could show Iberian origins for the Iron Age of southern Ireland, but it could also just mean that a very common form of European defence, using wooden stakes, was made in stone instead because of the lack of trees in the area.

The life-expectancy of an oak post in the ground has been calculated as fifteen years for each inch of radius, so a wooden *chevaux-de-frise* would need to be replaced after about forty-five years; stone would be far more durable.

One of the most important 'royal sites' is Navan Fort or Emain Macha, mentioned in the oldest Irish texts as the seat of the kings of Ulster. The diameter of the circular earthwork is about 230 metres, and it had a large bank and ditch. Remains of early Iron Age houses were found during excavation, and finds included metalwork of late Hallstatt type.

A great oak post, more than half-a-metre in diameter and dated to 94 BC, established the start of Celtic or Late Iron Age activity. This post, about 12 metres in height, marked the centre of a circular wooden building which seems to have been roofed. This building was packed with limestone blocks. The structure was then set on fire deliberately, and the resulting cairn was covered with a mound of cut turves. The building has been reconstructed at the site, and can be visited. Its design echoes a wheel, with radiating spokes, a common Celtic motif. The burning seems to have had a ritual function, possibly the re-enaction of a myth; the circular structure could have symbolised the wheel of the sun.

The date of the burning, however, is at least 500 years before the date given by historians to the final burning of Emain Macha. This is a long time for an oral tradition to have survived. Probably the archaeological evidence of the burning of one stage of use, and the description of a later destruction, are similar by accident. No metal objects were associated with the Iron Age remains of this fort, but among the finds was the skull of a Barbary ape, dated between 390 and 20 BC, which must have come originally from north Africa. Such an exotic import may demonstrate the important political role of this site.

Irish king, Celtic twilight version. Courtesy of Peter Costello.

Kingship

When the early Christian missionaries reached Ireland during the fifth century AD, they found a political system which consisted of about 150 'kings', each ruling a tribal area or *tuath*. None of these was what is called a 'high king', because that was a later historical development. The king seemed to act as a spiritual leader as well as a political one, and various clues hint at a kind of 'sacred marriage', when the king would be ceremoniously 'married' to the land he ruled. This would also imply that he had a role in the fertility of the land, and the prosperity of his people. An injured or maimed king could not rule.

The king was not necessarily the son of the previous king, but could be a member of his extended family. A king could be chosen

*The Petrie 'crown', a bronze headpiece, decorated in low
relief. The horn is hollow, of sheet bronze folded and
sealed. Photograph National Museum of Ireland.*

from any of the descendants of a common great-grandfather. Once
you no longer had a grandparent or great-grandparent who had been
king, you would no longer have any right to succeed. Succession
seems to have been a matter of the strongest of the available
candidates exerting his right by demonstrating his strength, possibly
with the agreement of the previous king on his deathbed.

We know of installation ceremonies for the kings of Tara (Co.
Meath), Navan Fort (Co. Armagh) and Cruachain (Co.
Roscommon); poets seem to have had a role in the ritual. These
centres of kingship may have been deliberately chosen as
continuations of pre-Celtic traditions; a number of them, such as
Knowth (Co. Meath), built on a massive passage tomb, were
connected with important Neolithic or Bronze Age sites.

Above: *Stone of Scone, now in Edinburgh Castle – ancient coronation seat of the Irish Celts brought to Scotland in the middle ages and captured there by the English. Photograph Historic Scotland.*

Below: *Induction ceremony of an Irish king as described by Giraldus Cambrensis; drawing by Susan Hayes after the original in the National Library of Ireland (NLI MS 700).*

The twelfth century Welshman, Giraldus Cambrensis, who came to Ireland with the Normans, has left us a horrified account of a royal inauguration ceremony in Tirconnell, in the north, during which the king mates with a mare, and subsequently baths in the water in which she was cooked. This is a very late survival, and Giraldus may have been passing on ancient legend rather than contemporary truth; he was certainly appalled by it.

The inauguration of the king of Tara in historic times was called by the term *Feis* which, translated as 'feast', also implies a fertility rite of some kind. This inauguration seems to have been originally a ritual marriage between the king and the goddess Medb. A standing stone at the site (an obvious phallic symbol, if you like), called the Lia Fáil or 'stone of destiny', played an important role in the ceremony. It was said to cry out, as a sign of whether the king being inaugurated was legitimate.

A great many references to the rights and duties of kingship appear in the Irish law tracts. If the king rules justly, the land will be prosperous; the three things which can cause the overthrow of a king are injustice, extortion and kin-slaying. Losing in battle is a sign of injustice, after which he can be deposed. A king was usually restricted by taboos, called *geisi*, supernatural prohibitions which he broke at his peril; it would a sign of injustice if he did. The laws were in the hands of a legal class, but it seems the king could issue occasional ordinances after, for example, a plague. He also may have had a role in law-enforcement, and could sit in judgement, or support judgements of the brehons or lawyers.

5

ART AND ARTEFACTS

General Survey

Most of the Irish material from the Celtic Iron Age was manufactured in Ireland. There are very few identifiable imports. Almost half of the surviving metal objects are horse-trappings, often showing signs of hard wear and frequent repair. We have few weapons, such as swords or spears, and no chariots. Of agricultural implements, there is one iron sickle, a few wooden ard-heads which were used for ploughing, and numerous quernstones for grinding corn.

The Broighter Hoard (see below) represents our main source of information about personal adornment. Of other decorative metalwork, some bronze trumpets survive, of possibly ritual function. There is no evidence of pottery, and no coinage. The burial rite was still simple cremation, as it had been for hundreds of years, and grave goods are sparse – a few pins, brooches and glass beads. Few tools are known, apart from the occasional axe or adze; the wooden trackway in Corlea demonstrates highly-developed woodworking skills, but no tools were found with it.

The rotary quern makes its first appearance during the Late Iron Age, possibly even as late as the second century AD. Two types are known, the beehive quern and the disc quern, distinguished by shape. One of the technological developments of the Iron Age, this

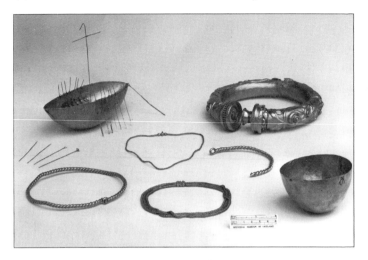

Broighter hoard. Photograph National Museum of Ireland
See also colour section.

method of grinding corn was operated with a wooden handle, and needed much less physical labour than the old rubbing-stones. It spread very rapidly through Europe.

In Ireland, no rotary quern was found on a settlement site; in fact, almost all those that we have were found in bogs, and showed very little sign of wear. It was possible that these were ritual deposits of some kind. They are only found in the northern part of the country. Anthropologists have found that in certain primitive societies, this kind of highly-efficient grinder is used by groups of people, rather than a single household. Its use may then imply some kind of change in the way work or society was organised.

As for other household materials of the Celtic Iron Age, there exist only a few tiny fragments of woven textile, some spindle whorls, scraps of worked leather, and bone objects such as combs and gaming-pieces. A small number of cauldrons have been found, the majority made of wood. Some, however, were of bronze. All were found buried at wetland sites.

The absence of pottery is a distinct puzzle. Plenty of pottery survived from the Late Bronze Age, mostly very coarse bucket-shaped ware, but pottery then disappears from the archaeological record from about 500 years BC until late in the first millennium AD, about 1000 years in all. A small amount of imported pottery has been found, including some Roman fragments. Clay moulds and crucibles must have been used for metal-working, although none of these have yet been found, so the knowledge of pottery didn't vanish completely. It must have just been considered unnecessary, when containers of metal, leather, wicker or wood could be used instead. A change of diet may have been involved, or different methods of food preparation. If the way of life was more nomadic than settled, following herds of cattle for example, pottery is awkward to carry or pack, compared to vessels of leather or wicker.

Metal-working

The Broighter Hoard, found in Lough Foyle and now kept in the National Museum, Dublin, provides us with art of unparalleled beauty and grace. It contained a large gold tubular collar with decorated terminals, two twisted gold bracelets, a delicate model of a boat in gold, two woven-chain gold necklets (of a familiar Roman type) and a gold bowl with four twisted ring-handles. The bracelets and necklets were probably imported from Britain or the continent. The collar may also be an import, but it certainly seems to have been decorated by an Irish artist, and is a masterpiece of the gold-worker's art.

The most delicate artefact in the hoard is the tiny nine-oared sailing boat, with its central mast, and a steering oar at the stern (*see colour section*). It probably represents a hide boat, which could be up to 20 metres in length. It would have had a square sail, and the model also includes an anchor, and a spar which may have been used to angle the sail towards the wind. Such hide boats, or currachs, have been used in Ireland for centuries.

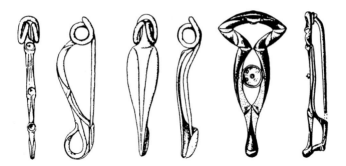

Above: *Drawings of fibula of various designs, items typical of Celtic life in Ireland and Europe.*
Below: *Ring-headed pin.*

The Somerset Hoard, another Iron Age collection, was found in Co. Galway in 1959. This contained three small cylindrical bronzes (two joined together to make a box); a twisted gold collar; two openwork bronze objects, one with traces of enamel; a fibula; a cup handle with a bird's head, also bronze; and two ingots of bronze. There seem to have been some iron objects also, but they were not preserved.

One of the most widespread types of Iron Age jewellery, in Britain and Europe, was the fibula, a type of safety-pin fastener whose surface was often decorated. However, only twenty-five or so of these are known in Ireland, almost all of them of Irish manufacture. The one uniquely Irish type (called the Navan fibula because some were found near Navan Fort) has a ball-and-socket mechanism for the pin, unknown anywhere else. Also numerous are bronze ringheaded pins; these are concentrated in Co. Antrim, where no fibulae at all have been found. Two mirrors have been found in Ireland, one of iron, on Lambay Island, Co. Dublin (probably imported) and one at Ballymoney, Co. Antrim.

The second largest category of finds from the Iron Age consists of almost fifty bronze spear-butts, which are common in Ireland and parts of Britain. These highly-decorated objects, fitted to the base of a spear-shaft, were probably objects of display, 'parade dress', so to speak. As for other military equipment, the iron swords which survive were short, thrusting weapons, about 38 cm. long on average. The iron tang would have been covered with a handle of bone or wood. Sword types were subject to changes in fashion, and the hilts and scabbards were good backgrounds for decoration and display. There are eight scabbards, some beautifully decorated. Some of the best British La Tène art occurs on huge bronze shields, but Ireland has so far revealed only one wooden leather-covered shield, made from alder wood, and one bronze shield-boss.

The only evidence for the use of chariots consists of one wooden yoke, two bronze mounts and a terret, apparently imported from Britain – a terret is a loop through which reins are passed. However, over one hundred horse-bits survive, and there are over ninety so-called 'pendants'. This name is given to a puzzling y-shaped

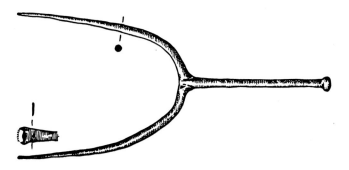

A mysterious y-shaped 'leader', Co. Antrim.

Above & below: *Iron-age horse bit in the National Museum of Ireland.*

article, which may have been used for leading a horse. These are only found in Ireland and nowhere else.

Four trumpets survive, made of bronze. They are masterpieces of sheet metalwork, quite unlike the cast bronze trumpets of the Late Bronze Age, and are decorated in the La Tène style. One was found at the lake of Loughnashade, just below Navan Fort; it seems to have been associated with human skulls, and may have been a votive or ritual deposit. The finest of the trumpets is that found at Ardbrin, Co. Down.

An interesting aspect of metal-working is the status given to a smith, which is often referred to in the later Old Irish law tracts. Iron was worked on almost every occupation site of Iron Age date that we can identify. Probably most farmers were able to carry out occasional ironworking, along with other manufactures such as basket-weaving or woodwork, but the specialist smith seems to have been highly respected. Even after the arrival of Christianity, the iron-smith had a magical or religious significance, and the forge was a focal point of the community. According to the Laws, news of a missing child or a straying horse had to be given to the smith, so that it could be passed on. In some legends, the smith played a ritual function on ceremonial occasions. In itself, iron was supposed to have magical powers, and even up to mediaeval times a hot iron was used in 'trial by ordeal', to discover the truth.

Work In Stone

Five identifiably Iron Age standing stones survive. These are covered with decoration which can be described as Celtic La Tène. There are other standing stones which are undecorated, but which can be dated to the Iron Age; there is an example at Tara, Co. Meath. Several Iron Age stone heads have been found; we are immediately reminded of classical descriptions of the head-hunting continental Celt.

None of the pillar stones can be associated with datable archaeological evidence, and the find-places of the occasional sculpted heads or human figures are randomly scattered over the country. The work was clearly designed and carried out in Ireland, but the question of outside influence remains unresolved. Comparisons have been made with standing stones in Brittany, but very few of those are decorated, and the ornament used is quite different. As for the heads, few of them can be properly dated, and many are associated with early Christian church-sites. They are

unlikely to date back before Romano-British influence. We can only use artistic criteria to place them, comparing them with datable heads from the continent. The most famous Irish head, which is accepted as Iron Age, is the three-faced stone head from Corleck, Co. Cavan (*see opposite*).

The most renowned of the Irish standing stones is the Turoe Stone, originally found near a small habitation site which may have been occupied in the Late Iron Age. The stone, weighing about four tons, is notable for the curvilinear patterns in relief which cover its upper section, and these are datable to not later than the first century BC. It can be compared to insular metalwork of the period; the artist had a repertoire which expressed wider European influences in an Irish style. It is probable that this sophisticated style was also developed in wood, and that carved wooden pillars were part of the artistic heritage; they would not of course have survived.

Stone bears, Cathedral Hill, Armagh. Photograph Ulster Museum.

Wood-working

Over the years, occasional wooden carvings of human figures have been found in Britain and Ireland, but these could not be dated until the development of radiocarbon dating, using a technique called Accelerator Mass Spectrometry. The best-known Irish example is the figure from Ralaghan, Co. Cavan, which was first described in 1930, although the find date is not known. It was carved from yew, and found in a bog. It is almost 1 m. tall, and its radiocarbon date is between 1096 and 906 BC (*see opposite*). Another wooden figure, found in Lagore crannóg, was previously assumed to be of early Christian date, but its radiocarbon date is much too old for that. However, if it was made of ancient wood found in a bog, as sometimes happened, the date would be distorted. It is Iron Age in style.

The one Iron Age shield we have, as mentioned above, is of alder wood, covered in leather and rectangular in shape. An imported wooden tankard, bound in bronze, was found at Carrickfergus, Co. Antrim, and there is a large cauldron of poplar wood from Co. Monaghan. Five wooden vessels with handles have survived, and many fragments of wooden vessels were found during the excavations at the Corlea trackway. The earliest evidence of wheeled transport in Ireland consists of two huge wooden block-wheels, of about 400 BC, which were found at Doogarymore, Co.

Doogarrymore wheel. Photograph National Museum of Ireland.

Roscommon, in the 1960s. The best-preserved one was made of three lengths of thick plank, of alder wood, fastened edge-to-edge by two large dowels made of yew. The wheel revolved on an axle, which passed through a circular opening (with a long wooden sleeve) in the central plank.

Artistic Style

On continental Europe, La Tène art was going into decline by the first century BC. However, in Britain and Ireland it was reaching unparalleled heights of virtuosity. The compass had not been used on the continent since the early La Tène period, but the curved and

La Tène carved granite boulder, Castlestrange,
Co. Roscommon, 2nd – 1st century BC. Photograph Don Sutton.

To the Greeks a spiral is a spiral and a face a face, and it is always clear where the one ends and the other begins, whereas the Celts 'see' the faces 'into' the spirals or tendrils: ambiguity is a characteristic of Celtic art...it is full of contrasts. It is attractive and repellent, it is far from primitiveness and simplicity; it is refined in thought and technique, elaborate and clever, full of paradoxes, restless, puzzlingly ambiguous; rational and irrational; dark and uncanny...

P. Jacobstahl, *Early Celtic Art*, Oxford 1944

circular patterns which it helped to create became a trademark of British and Irish La Tène art.

Irish La Tène art reached its climax in the first century AD. Good examples of its quality are found on a small group of

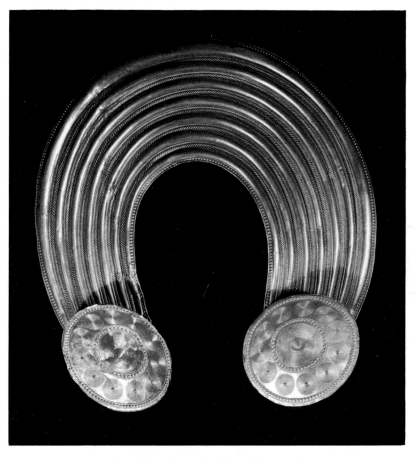

*Gold collar, Gleninsheen, Co. Clare. Photograph
National Museum of Ireland.*

elaborately-decorated bronze discs (use unknown), ornamented
with *repoussé* curves, that is, curves raised in relief by hammering
from behind. These bear comparison anywhere in the world as
masterpieces of non-representational art. Most of them have no
find-place, but two come from Monasterevin, Co. Kildare, so the
discs are called 'Monasterevin type'. Further examples of this type

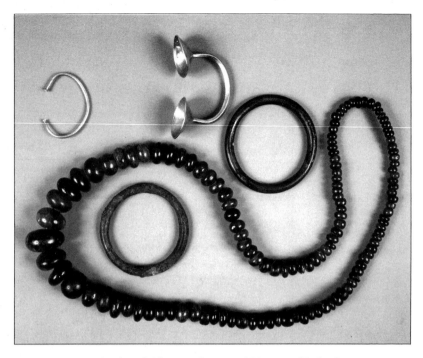

Banagher hoard. Photograph National Museum of Ireland.

of art are found on the Loughnashade trumpets, the Bann scabbards, and a bronze disc from the River Bann.

The essence of this art was simplicity, a spare use of balanced curves. It has been described as ambiguous, full of contrasts; many patterns can be seen more than one way, yet retain their perfect balance and harmony. It is a mixture of abstract designs such as curves and spirals, added to by shapes taken from nature: leaves, bird beaks, owl eyes. For me, as for many people, La Tène art has always represented a pinnacle of artistic expression, completely satisfying to the eye. It is better seen than described, as the

Opposite: *Neolithic (New Stone Age) worked flint macehead (2,500 BC), found in the passage tomb of knowth, Co. Meath. The Irish Celts adopted the ancient spiral motif into their own style of art.*

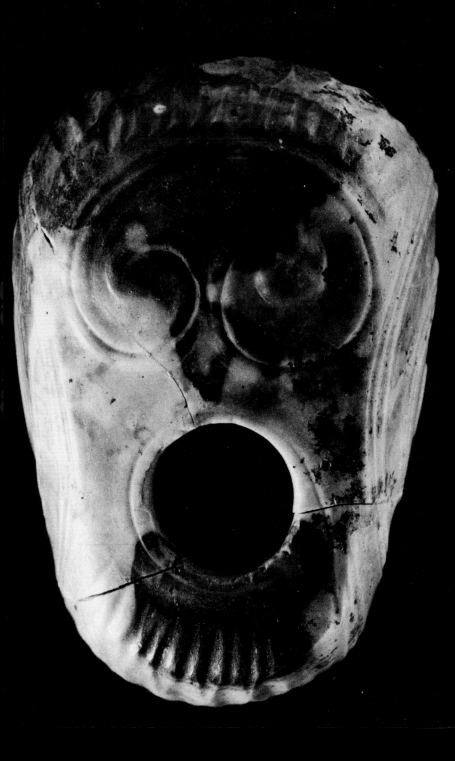

illustrations here show. We will never know what deeper symbolism these designs may have contained; Australian aboriginal abstract paintings, for example, can contain hidden references to a 'Dreamtime' mythological tale, or to specific placenames.

While Roman influences began to affect the La Tène style in Britain, Ireland remained isolated, and the continuity of Irish La Tène art stayed more or less intact until the coming of Christianity, although there was of course some overseas influence. Small bronze objects such as boxes and pins, and gold jewellery such as brooches, continued to be decorated with La Tène motifs – bird-heads, trefoil patterns, S-shaped curves. The influence of such patterns passed down through the centuries, and can still be seen in the illuminated manuscript masterpieces, created several hundred years after the original development of La Tène art.

Extract from Londonderry Ordnance Survey Memoirs, 1835
Parish Aghadowey. 'Bog of Ballybritain anciently called Muttonhole. Almost forty years ago a man and a boy were cutting turf when there suddenly fell out from beneath their spades a heathen image or god so hideous that the boy, a weak sickly lad, fainted with horror. It was a long circular block of wood like the trunk of a tree and about six feet long, at the top there were four heads looking opposite ways with four faces and carved hair. The elder of the labourers immediately set it up on his garden-wall, where multitudes of country-people flocked to see it. After a few months, by the action of the weather, it decayed and fell to pieces. It probably served as an excellent scarecrow. Many of the parishioners recollect seeing it, and can still accurately describe it.'

6

THE EVIDENCE OF WRITTEN SOURCES

Acht ropa airderc-sa, maith lim cenco beind acht oenla for domun
(Provided I be famous, I am content to be only one day on earth)
CU CHULAINN

Nineteenth-century antiquarians, in thrall to the Celtic Twilight, saw the Irish Iron Age through the window of myths and legends, great Irish sagas such as the Ulster Cycle, which had been preserved in ancient manuscripts. These tales portrayed a hierarchical warrior society, ruled by kings, with an important caste of druids and poets, and a highly-developed legal system. To a great extent they were taken as unquestioned fact, but nowadays, how far these stories can be used as evidence of Iron Age culture is a source of much discussion.

The tales were based on an oral tradition, and were not written down until at least the seventh century AD, when the early Christian monks began to collect them. Oral tradition can preserve stories unchanged for generations, but there is always a risk that aspects of a tale will be gradually altered, or left out as their meaning becomes lost, or as tastes change. The monks were not necessarily accurate recorders either. They censored material which they considered pagan or obscene, and were naturally influenced, knowingly or not, by the times in which they wrote. For instance, the long slashing swords described in the Ulster Cycle as we have it bear no relation to the swords which we know actually date to the Iron Age. They sound much more like the Viking-influenced swords which were in use during the period the monks were writing in.

Even while the original tales were being told, they were coming under the influence of classical Greek and Roman writings, of the Scriptures and of other early Christian religious sources. So how much of the original, pre-Christian, indigenous foundation remains?

The Ulster Cycle, a massive and dramatic saga, contains at least eighty separate stories, including such great tales of old Irish literature as The Cattle-Raid of Cooley (*Táin Bó Cuailgne*), Deirdre and the Sons of Uisneach, and so on. The *Táin* or Cattle-Raid tale is centred around Ulster, and deals with a great war between Ulster and Connacht; Ulster was certainly a dominant kingdom in late Iron Age Ireland, until the middle of the fifth century AD.

The oldest surviving version of the Táin (called Recension I) is found in two manuscripts: the *Book of the Dun Cow* or *Lebor na hUidhre*, an eleventh century compilation now in the Royal Irish Academy, Dublin; and the *Yellow Book of Lecan*, a fourteenth century compilation. This version is thought to be based on two lost ninth-century versions, and some scholars believe that the tale was first written down as far back as the seventh century. There is also a fuller version of the tale, known as Recension II, written in the late twelfth century and preserved in the *Book of Leinster*, which is now in Trinity College Dublin.

Scribe from Giraldus, drawn by
Susan Hayes, after a MSS in the
National Library of Ireland.

The opening of the ancient Irish epic, The Táin, *recounting the cattle raid*
of Cooley and the defence of Ulster by Cuchulain.

'Another company came to the hill at Slemain Midi,' Mac Roth said. 'It seemed greater than a troop of three thousand, with a white-breasted, well-favoured warrior at its head, who looked like Ailill in size and handsomeness and apparel. He wore a gold crown on his head, and a red-embroidered tunic. A cloak of great beauty wrapped him round, fastened on the breast with a gold brooch. He carried a gold-rimmed, death-dealing shield and a spear like the pillar of a palace. A gold-hilted sword hung at his shoulder.'

Táin Bó Cuailgne (trans. by Thomas Kinsella)

'It behoves you to act warily with yon man, little lad,' said Ibar. 'Why is that?' said the boy [Cu Chulainn]. 'The man you see is Foill mac Nechtain. No points nor weapons nor sharp edges harm him.' 'Not to me should you say that, Ibar,' said the boy. 'I shall take in hand for him my *deil cliss*, that is, the round ball of refined iron, and it will land on the flat of his shield and the flat of his forehead and carry out through the back of his head a portion of brain equal to the iron ball, and he will be holed like a sieve so that the light of the air will be visible through his head.' Foill mac Nechtain came forth. Cu Chulainn took in hand for him the *deil cliss*, and hurled it so that it landed on the flat of his shield and the flat of his forehead and took the ball's equivalent of his brains through the back of his head, and he was holed like a sieve so that the light of the air was visible through his head. And Cu Chulainn struck off his head from his neck.

Táin Bó Cuailgne, edited and translated by Cecile O'Rahilly.

Then his first distortion came upon Cu Chulainn so that he became horrible, many-shaped, strange and unrecognisable. His haunches shook about him like a tree in a current or a bulrush against a stream, every limb and every joint, every end and every member of him from head to foot. He performed a wild feat of contortion with his body inside his skin. His feet and his shins and his knees came to the back; his heels and his calves and his hams came to the front. The sinews of his calves came on the front of his shins and each huge, round knot of them was as big as a warrior's fist...He sucked one of his eyes into his head so that a wild crane could hardly have reached it to pluck it out from the back of his skull on to the middle of his cheek. The other eye sprang out on to his cheek. His mouth was twisted back fearsomely. He drew the cheek back from the jawbone until his inner gullet was seen. His lungs and his liver fluttered in his mouth and his throat...

Táin Bó Cuailgne, O'Rahilly translation.

Also beyond counting were Conchobor's household and his houses. There were one hundred and fifty inner rooms, each of which held three couples. The houses and rooms were panelled with red yew. In the centre of the house was Conchobor's own room, guarded by screens of copper, with bars of silver and gold birds on the screens, and precious jewels in the birds' heads for eyes. Over Conchobor's head was a rod of silver with three apples of gold, for keeping order over the throng. If it shook, or he raised his voice, everyone fell into such a respectful silence you would hear a needle drop to the floor. At any given time in Conchobor's room there were thirty noble heroes drinking out of Gerg's vat, which was always kept full.

Tain Bó Cuailgne, Kinsella translation.

Internal evidence shows that the Ulster Cycle has pre-Christian roots, dating back maybe a hundred years before Christianity came. This is still a long way after the La Tène Iron Age of the Celts. The stories may have been idealising a period long past, with little relation to reality. The Ulster Cycle has a lot to say about religious beliefs, and is of great interest to people who study the development of language and literature, but the archaeologist has to treat this kind of material very cautiously indeed. The type of society described in the Ulster Cycle is very close in many respects to continental Celtic society around 100 BC, as described in classical sources. This could mean that both societies developed separately, from a far-distant shared Indo-European source, or that continental Celts came directly to Ireland in the last few centuries BC.

The Ulster Cycle portrays a heroic warrior society, and very close parallels can be drawn with the accounts of the Celts that we find in such writers as Posidonius. His work cannot have been known to the seventh and eighth century Irish writers, but these writers echo many of his details extremely closely. The ruling caste in the Ulster Cycle are called the Ulaid, and they rule from Emain Macha (now Navan Fort). The heroes fight from chariots, like the Homeric Greeks, and spend their lives hunting and feasting. Ptolemy, writing in the second century AD, refers to the Ulaid, and the placename 'Isamnion' in his description of Ireland may refer to Emain Macha.

Legal Texts

Another possible written source for information on the Celtic Iron Age is the surviving law tracts. In historical times, the Irish laws were upheld and transmitted by a class of learned men known as *brehons*, although the *filidh* or poets also acted as custodians of tradition. It is probable that both these classes had taken over the functions which used to belong to druids, although we know very little about the presence or activities of druids in Ireland.

The law texts, called the Brehon Laws, were first written down

A son begotten on a chief wife in defiance of her husband, the fosterage falls on the man who commits the outrage, and not alone that, but he pays body-fine and honour-price to the man whose wife she is. Moreover, the child is the property of the woman's husband until bought from him, and fosterage fee is due from the man whose child it is if he delays without buying him until he is past the age of fosterage, unless it is by capture the child has been taken from him.

If the husband leaves his wife and proclaims that no man should take her and a son is begotten on her and he takes her back, she is not bound to pay a fosterage-fee or to share the fosterage.

If it is while there is strife [between her and her husband] that she is got with child by the man, or if her husband has surrendered her – but not to that man; or if the husband put her away and then took her again; the offspring begotten while she is away, he will not [have to] bring it up, for it was begotten in spite of her husband's prohibition.

From *Cáin Lánamna*, 'Marriage Law', which is contained in *Senchas Már* ('the great old knowledge'), a compilation of law tracts made during the eighth century AD.

Horse and wheel. Boic silver coin. Diameter 2.5cm. National Museum, Budapest, Hungary. Photograph AKG London, by Erich Lessing.

in Old Irish in the seventh and eighth centuries. However, most of them have only been transmitted to us in late manuscripts, of the fourteenth to sixteenth centuries. They were heavily footnoted and added to in the seventh and eighth centuries, in order to bring them up date with the existing legal system, and the influence of Roman law can also be detected, but the basic texts date back to a more primitive time. These tracts are astonishingly close in some ways to Hindu law, showing the common Indo-European roots of both.

Interestingly, the society shown in the law tracts is not an heroic society at all; it is based on mixed farming – cattle, sheep, pigs, cereals – and there is no warrior status. The levels of social class include kings, lords and professional men such as poets, judges, doctors and blacksmiths. Tribal law and custom had been diligently preserved for a long time, orally, by a professional class of poets. These took advantage of the literacy brought by Christianity to copper-fasten their authority. They wrote down the strict rules and regulations which limited the power of even the most powerful king, and forbade any change to be made.

There is detailed information on such customs as 'fasting' (a type of hunger-strike) as a method of gaining justice, and of 'clientship', which is a relationship binding a man to his lord. There was a complicated organisation of suretyship. A man of high status could stand surety for someone of lower class, and each social class had its own 'honour-price'. A man's honour-price, what he was considered to be worth, was the amount due to him if he were injured in any way, and was also what was paid to his family if he was killed. If he dishonoured his status, his honour-price would be lowered, or removed completely, leaving him without legal standing.

The family was the basis of society, and kinship obligations were strictly laid down and enforced. People were aware of their family up to quite distant degrees of relationship, and degrees of kinship were important for such matters as inheritance and marriage. Marriage laws permitted divorce, and the law also recognised transient sexual unions, and the taking of a second wife, or a concubine. The position of women in these early laws seems to have

Maiden and warrior in the idealised version of the Celtic twilight poets.
Courtesy of Peter Costello.

When a husband takes a concubine:

The *cetmuinter* [first or head wife] is entitled to do anything until the end of three nights, save to inflict death; if she inflicts death restitution [only] is due from her, and half fine is payable by her [for all assaults] from that on. The *adaltrach* [concubine] is free from liability up to [except for] shedding blood till the end of three nights, and full fine is due from her immediately for shedding blood, and half fine for death up to three nights, and full fine after that always.

The *cetmuintir* is completely free from liability for anything she may do during the first three nights short of killing, and retribution is due from her for killing...

Cáin Lánamna

permitted a degree of independence, and of personal property which a husband, for example, could not make use of without consent. However, the laws as we have them reflect hundreds of years of social development, and it is impossible to be sure which laws existed side by side, and which are later additions, under Roman or Christian influence.

The picture of society the laws show us is highly uniform and stylised, with a passion for classification. There must have been a lot of local differences, and most of the classifications of tiny, minor details would never have been used in practical day-to-day law. This written-down law was ancient, originally based on custom, and guarded by lawyers or jurists who would not permit any alteration or modernisation; it was fossilised.

Ogham

The ogham script should be mentioned here, although it was very late in development. The earliest ogham markings we have date to the fourth century AD, and it was used up to about the eighth century AD. This script, consisting of strokes or notches which were cut

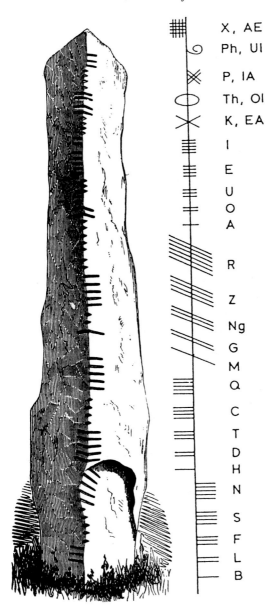

X, AE
Ph, UI
P, IA
Th, OI
K, EA
I
E
U
O
A
R
Z
Ng
G
M
Q
C
T
D
H
N
S
F
L
B

Far left:
*Monataggart
ogham stone.
Coffey
catalogue.*

Left: *Ogham
script
alphabet.
Courtesy of
Peter
Costello.*

into wood, or along the edge of a standing stone, used the Roman alphabet. It was a clumsy method of marking, based on groups of one to five strokes for each letter, and was used only for short inscriptions, such as grave markers or memorials.

The names found on these markers are definitely Celtic in form. Typical inscriptions are GRILAGNI MAQI SCILAGNI (Grilagnos son of Scilagnos) from a stone in Co. Cork, and MAQI CAIRATINI AVI INEQAGLASI (Mac Cairthinn, grandson of Enechglass), a later example from Leinster. Over 300 of these inscriptions are known in Ireland, mostly in the southern part of the country. It is speculated that the script is much older than it seems, and was originally based on a type of sign-language used by druids, using the five fingers.

The Geasas (or prohibitions) laid on King Conaire
(from Togail Bruidhne Da Derga)

Birds shall be privileged, and this should be your observance always: you shall not pass Tara on your right hand and Brega on your left; you shall not hunt the crooked beasts of Cernae, and you shall not stay abroad from Tara for nine nights; and you shall not spend the night in a house from which firelight is visible outside after sunset and into which one can see from outside; and three red men shall not go before you into a red man's house; and plunder shall not be taken during your reign; the visit of one woman shall not come into your house after sunset; and you shall not settle a quarrel between two of your subjects.

King Conaire's death took place after he had been forced to break every one of these prohibitions, by a series of coincidences.

Poem, from twelfth century Book of Leinster

Three things that are best for a prince during his reign are truth, mercy and silence; those that are worst for a king's honour are straying from the truth and adding to the false...Truth in a prince is as bright as the foam cast up by a mighty wave of the sea, as the sheen of a swan's covering in the sun, as the colour of snow on a mountain...A prince's truth is an effort which overpowers armies: it brings milk into the world, it brings corn and mast.

In Hindu tradition, the gods were born of truth and acted by means of truth, and the earth was supported by truth: 'By means of truth the sun is warm, by means of truth the moon shines, by means of truth the wind blows, by means of truth the world is stable...'

Bronze head of the statue of a Celtic god with glass-paste eye, from the oppidum at Bouray-sur-Juine, France. Photograph AKG London, by Erich Lessing.

7

SUMMING-UP

The question of how and when the Celts arrived in Ireland may never be satisfactorily answered. Obviously they did arrive, in some numbers, bringing their language and aspects of their culture, but we cannot be more specific.

It has often been argued that such a warlike people must have invaded, in force, from somewhere in Europe, and conquered the indigenous peoples who had lived in Ireland since the middle stone age. But the sparse archaeological record provides very little evidence for a massive invasion. Supporters of 'invasion' theories are convinced that aggressive armies must have arrived in Ireland in the early centuries AD, setting up new ruling dynasties and submerging the existing population. They say this is the most likely way in which a new language and culture could be introduced, and argue that what little evidence exists can be taken more than one way.

Most modern archaeological thinking is more inclined to contend that the Celts arrived gradually, in successive waves, spreading slowly across the country. This process could have taken several hundred years. Certainly by the dawn of history in Ireland, that is the arrival of Christianity in the fifth century AD, a Celtic language was being spoken all over the island, and there was a fairly uniform political system.

The spread of Celtic influence seems to have been very slow and

> Why is there so much fine [Bronze Age] metalwork to study? It was not created in order to provide material for doctoral theses, and the quantity and quality of these objects undermine the argument that much of it was lost by accident...Once we accept that it was deposited deliberately, we can turn our attention to those periods in which comparable material is under-represented. Where, for instance, is the missing *La Tène* metalwork? Perhaps we have identified these gaps because we expect metal artefacts to be evenly distributed through time, but again that may be an unreasonable expectation. The large-scale deposition of valuables could have been fairly short-lived. It was a specific social tradition, and in the south it seems to have possessed a particularly local character...Traditions of deposition (or non-deposition) may highlight local differences of culture just as effectively as the stylistic analysis of artefacts.
>
> Twohig and Ronayne, *Perceptions of the Past*

gradual. There is no evidence for sudden incursions of warriors, sweeping all before them and wiping out the native population. Insofar as anything is clear about this period, the already existing Irish population must have found itself confronted by groups of people of British or European Celtic origin. These arrivals may have started coming as far back as the late Bronze Age. Various waves of small groups may then have kept on coming, as population movements continued to push west in Europe.

Perhaps continental Celtic groups followed rumours of a fertile land to the west; perhaps they had maintained family or tribal contacts with earlier emigrants, and followed on when they were forced to. It seems clear that the incoming Celtic groups were more wealthy or technologically advanced than the natives, and were able to wield an influence out of proportion to their numbers, otherwise Celtic would hardly have become the majority language.

A starting-point of sometime before 1000 BC could be given for the first contact of a Celtic language with Ireland. For instance, there would not have been much linguistic difference between Britain and Ireland, because parts of both islands were in close and frequent contact, although there may have been wide variations of dialect. Among many peoples, even in primitive societies, the use of more than one language for different circumstances or communicating with different groups is quite commonplace. The late Bronze Age, early Iron Age and late Iron Age could have seen very important linguistic changes being brought about by relatively small groups of people.

Social change and language change are closely linked. If a particular language or dialect is linked with high social status, with wealth and power, it will be imitated by the people on the lower levels who wish to raise their own status. This will only work if there is social interaction between the social classes, from one level to another, so that the élites come into contact with the lower levels, and both sides have to make themselves understood. Certainly, the very stratified society described in the Old Irish laws, in which both upper and lower classes had clearly-defined rights and duties in relation to each other, would provide such an interaction. Without it, the society could not have functioned. Eventually, the language of the élite will dominate all other dialects.

This kind of fundamental change need not leave any archaeological evidence behind at all. It is known historically, for example, that in the late fifth century AD, Irish colonisers swept into Scotland from Ulster and established the kingdom of Dal Riata in the south-west. From here, their Goidelic language spread until it had covered all of Scotland by about 1000 AD. But there is no *archaeological* evidence for this series of events, covering almost 600 years, which changed the face of Scotland completely.

Part of the difficulty in dealing with non-linguistic evidence lies in the fact that most of the Iron Age material does not have a proper archaeological context, a find-spot that can be scientifically excavated and dated. Isolated discoveries, falling out of bogs or fished out of rivers, often damaged by people who did not recognise them as important, give us no direct information about their

> When archaeologists abandon their proper domain and indulge
> in linguistic speculations, the precariousness of their theorizings
> is increased ten-fold...'The natural desire to bring objects of
> archaeological interest into relation with communities known
> from documentary evidence...leads frequently to a severe strain
> on the credulity of the layman,' writes John Fraser. And again:
> 'The principle that it is dangerous...to argue that [a man's]
> language must have been this or that because his skull was of a
> particular shape and his weapons of a particular pattern, is
> generally recognized, but is not always acted on. No one would
> dream of applying such tests in the case of a living man; and the
> mere fact that the object of investigation has been dead for
> thousands of years, and that no other tests *can* be applied, cannot
> make the results of this method any more convincing.'
>
> T.F. O'Rahilly, *Early Irish History and Mythology*

manufacture or date. Obviously, if you turn up something buried in
a field that gleams gold when you scratch it, you will guess it is
valuable, but a lump of corroded iron will be thrown aside. Iron is
easily destroyed in poor conditions, and even a well-preserved iron
artefact doesn't necessarily look good enough to bring home and
display.

Generally, a poor tenant finding a valuable object in a field would
be afraid of having it confiscated by the authorities, and would just
bring it straight to a jeweller, giving no information about where the
object was found. The valuable would then be melted down, and
disappear forever. It was only during the nineteenth century that
'antiquarians', usually educated gentlemen with time on their
hands, began to take an interest in the past, seeking out 'antiquities'
and recording any information about them they could find.

However meagre and unsatisfactory the archaeological record is,
it can always be improved. At any time some new discovery,
whether randomly on a seashore or the result of planned, meticulous
excavation, can turn well-founded theories upside down, unsettle
reliable chronologies, and send everyone back to the

drawing-board. For the Irish Iron Age, we have too many random, casual finds with no definite find-spot or dating. Possibly specific, targeted excavation at chosen sites may enlarge our information.

The information we already have can also be subjected to different types of investigation. Anthropological evidence from primitive communities, for example, can be used to test theories of Celtic social and religious organisation. The old mythical stories of Ireland's origin speak of the country as being divided into 'Five Fifths', that is the four existing provinces of Ulster, Munster, Leinster and Connacht, and a fifth, dominant, province, in the middle, called Midhe (Meath). These 'five fifths' might represent some sort of (?druidic) cosmological scheme rather than a real, physical division of regions. Ancient Indo-European societies often had rigid caste systems of social function, symbolised by geographical divisions.

A strong strand in Indo-European religion is the belief in lucky and unlucky places, or dates, or points of the compass, as can be seen on the Calendar of Coligny discussed above. Perhaps more can be learned about religious beliefs by studying whether fort or house entrances face east or west, or how burials are arranged. Unfortunately, even this kind of evidence is very thin on the ground in Ireland.

A certain amount of archaeological research has been done in Britain into the idea of 'household space' symbolism – that is, the notion that certain activities are restricted to certain areas of the house, for symbolic reasons. This kind of thinking can be found in societies all over the world; in Thailand, for example, the north is 'royal', the east is 'life-giving', and the west is 'unlucky'. In Britain, Iron Age houses almost invariably face east, towards the equinox or the sunrise, or southeast, towards the mid-winter solstice. Household activities are kept separate from one another – a living area, where weaving could be carried on, is separated from the cooking area, or from craft activities such as woodwork, and these divisions seem to follow a precise pattern. Another example of symbolic direction is provided by the Iron Age burials of the

Durotrigian tribe, in Britain, which contain sheep bones in graves facing south and east, but pig bones in graves facing northwest or west. What is the meaning behind this division?

We are nowhere near the end of what remains to be discovered about the Celts in Ireland, but we have to accept that there is a great deal we will probably never know. And the ultimate paradox is that, to quote Barry Raftery, 'in this most "Celtic" of islands, the material remains of the earliest "Celts" have yet to be found'.

> To many, perhaps to most people outside the small company of the great scholars, past and present, 'Celtic' of any sort is...a magic bag, into which anything may be put, and out of which almost anything may come...Anything is possible in the fabulous Celtic twilight, which is not so much a twilight of the gods as of the reason.
>
> J.R.R. TOLKIEN

*Celtic stone head, Armagh Cathedral. Photograph Robert Vance.
Courtesy Don Sutton Photo Library.*

BIBLIOGRAPHY

Binchy, D.A.,*Celtic and Anglo-Saxon Kingship* (O'Donnell Lecture), Clarendon Press, Oxford, 1970
The Linguistic and Historical Value of the Irish Law, Tracts (Sir John Rhys Memorial Lecture), British Academy, Vol. xxix, 1943
Studies in Early Irish Law (ed.), Royal Irish Academy, 1936

Bourke, Cormac (ed.), *From the Isles of the North*, Belfast, HMSO, 1995

Brailsford, J., *Early Celtic Masterpieces from Britain*, British Museum, 1975

Byrne, F.J., *Irish Kings and High-Kings*, London, 1973

Caesar, Julius, *The Conquest of Gaul*, transl. S.A. Handford, Penguin, 1963

Carey, M and Warmington, E.H., The Anceint Explorers, London, 1929 (Penguin, 1963)

Chadwick, Nora, *The Celts*, Penguin, 1970
The Druids, University of Wales Press, 1966

Champion, T.C., The Myth of Iron Age Invasions in Ireland, in Scott, *Studies in Early Ireland*

Champion, T.C. and Collis, J.R. (eds.), *The Iron Age in Britain and Ireland: Recent Trends*, Sheffield, 1996

Coffey, George, *Guide to the Celtic Antiquities of the Christian Period preserved in National Museum, Dublin*, Dublin 1909

Coles, B., Anthropomorphic wooden figurines from Britain and Ireland, *Proceedings of the Prehistoric Society*, Vol. 56, 1990

Cooney, G. and Grogan, E., An Archaeological Solution to the 'Irish Problem'?, *Emania* Vol. 9, 1991

Cunliffe, Barry, *The Celtic World*, Constable, 1992
Iron Age Communities in Britain, London, 1991

de Paor, Liam, *The Peoples of Ireland*, Hutchinson, 1986

Delaney, Frank, *The Celts*, 1986

Dillon, Myles, *The Archaism of Irish Tradition* (Sir John Rhys Memorial Lecture), University of Chicago, 1969
Early Irish Society, Dublin, 1954

Dillon, Myles and Chadwick, Nora, *The Celtic Realms*

Edwards, N. and Lane, *The Early Church in Wales and the West*, Oxbow Monographs, 1992

Eluère, Christine, *The Celts – First Masters of Europe*, Thames & Hudson, 1973

Eogan, George, *The Accomplished Art – Gold and Gold-Working in Britain and Ireland during the Bronze Age*, Oxford, 1994

Fox, Sir Cyril, *Pattern and Purpose: a survey of Early Celtic Art in Britain*, Cardiff, 1958

Frey, O.-H., Palmette and Circle: Early Celtic Art in Britain and its Continental Background, *Proceedings of the Prehistoric Society* Vol. 42, 1976

Glob, P.V., *The Bog People*, Paladin, 1971

Green, Miranda J. (ed.), *The Celtic World*, Routledge, 1995

Hamlin, A. and Lynn, C., *Pieces of the Past*, Belfast, HMSO, 1988

Harbison, Peter, *Pre-Christian Ireland: from the first settlers to the Early Celts*, Thames & Hudson, 1988
Wooden and Stone Chevaux-de-Frise, *Proceedings of the Prehistoric Society*, Vol. 37, 1971

Harding, D.W. (ed.), *Hillforts: later prehistoric earthworks*, London, 1976

Hawkes, C.F.C., The Wearing of the Brooch: Early Iron Age dress among the Irish, in Scott, *Studies in Early Ireland*

Henry, Francoise, *Irish Art in the Early Christian Period to A.D. 800*, London, 1965

Jackson, K.H., *A Celtic Miscellany*, Penguin Books, 1971
The Oldest Irish Tradition: A Window on the Iron Age, Cambridge, 1964

James, S, *Exploring the World of the Celts*, London, 1993

Joyce, P.W., *A Social History of Ancient Ireland*, London, 1903

Kelly, E.P., *Early Celtic Art in Ireland*, National Museum of Ireland, 1993

Kelly, Fergus, *A Guide to Early Irish Law*, Dublin Institute for Advanced Studies, 1988

Kinsella, Thomas (trans.), *The Táin*, Oxford, 1970

Koch, J.T., Eriu, Alba and Letha: When was a Language Ancestral to Gaelic first spoken in Ireland?, *Emania* Vol. 9, 1991

Kruta, V., Frey, O.-H., Raftery, B., Szabo, M. (eds.), *The Celts*, London, 1991

Laing, Lloyd & Jennifer, *Art of the Celts*, Thames and Hudson, 1992

Lang, J., The Technology of Celtic Iron Swords, in Scott and Cleere, *Crafts of the Blacksmith*

Leerssen, Joep, *Remembrance and Imagination: Patterns in Historical and Literary Representations of Ireland in the 19th c.*, Cork University Press 1996

Lucas, A.T., Prehistoric Block-Wheels from Doogarymore, Co. Roscommon and Timahoe East, Co. Kildare, *Jnl. Royal Society of Antiquaries* Vol. 102, 1972

Lynn, C.J., The Dorsey and other Linear Earthworks, in Scott, *Studies in Early Ireland*
Navan Fort – home of gods and goddesses?, *Archaeology Ireland*, Vol. 7:1, 1993

MacCana, Proinsias, *Celtic Mythology*, Hamlyn, 1970

MacNeill, Maire, *The Festival of Lughnasa*, Oxford University Press, 1962

Mallory, J.P., *Aspects of the Táin* (ed.), Belfast, 1992
The Origins of the Irish, *Journal of Irish Archaeology*, Vol. II, 1984
Two Perspectives on the Problem of Irish Origins, *Emania*, Vol. 9, 1991

Mallory, J.P. and McNeill, T.E. (eds.), *The Archaeology of Ulster*, Belfast, 1991

Megaw, R. and V., *Celtic Art from its beginnings*, Thames & Hudson, 1989

Murphy, G., *Saga and Myth in Ancient Ireland*, Dublin, 1961

Newman, Conor, The Iron Age to Early Christian Transition: The Evidence from Dress Fasteners, in Bourke, *From the Isles of the North*

O'Brien, Elizabeth, Pagan and Christian Burial in Ireland during the first Millennium AD: Continuity and Change, in Edwards & Lane, *Early Church*

O Corrain, D. (ed.), *Irish Antiquity*, Tower Books, 1981 [Four Courts, 1994]

O Floinn, Raghnall, Irish Bog Bodies, *Archaeology Ireland*, Vol. 2:3, 1988

O'Kelly, Michael J., *Early Ireland*, Cambridge, 1989

O'Rahilly, Cecile (ed.), *Táin Bó Cuailgne, from the Book of Leinster*, Dublin Institute for Advanced Studies, 1984

O'Rahilly, T.F., *Early Irish History and Mythology*, Dublin, 1946

O'Riordain, Sean, *Antiquities of the Irish Countryside*, London, 1953

Purdy, B.A. (ed.), *Wet Site Archaeology*, New Jersey, 1988

Raftery, Barry, *Catalogue of Irish Iron Age Antiquities*, Marburg, 1983
The Celtic Iron Age in Ireland: Problems of Origin, *Emania* Vol. 9, 1991
La Tène in Ireland – Problems of Origin and Chronology, Marburg, 1984
Pagan Celtic Ireland, Thames & Hudson, 1994
Sites and Sights of the Iron Age (ed.), Oxbow Monograph, 1995
Trackways Through Time, Headline, 1990

Raftery, Joseph, The Turoe Stone and the Rath of Feerwore, *Journal of Royal Society of Antiquaries of Ireland*, Vol. 74, 1944

Richter, Michael, *Medieval Ireland, The Enduring Tradition*, Gill and Macmillan, 1988

Ross, A., *Pagan Celtic Britain*, 1967

Ryan, Michael, *Treasures of Ireland – Irish Art 3000 BC-1500 AD* (ed.), Royal Irish Academy, 1983

Rynne, Etienne., *Figures from the Past* (ed.), Glendale Press, 1987
Celtic Stone Idols, in Thomas, *The Iron Age in the Irish Sea Province*

Scott, B.G., *Early Irish Ironworking*, Ulster Museum, 1990
The Status of the Blacksmith in Early Ireland in Scott and Cleere, *Crafts of the Blacksmith*
Studies in Early Ireland: Essays for Michael Duignan (ed.), Belfast, 1982

Scott, B.G. and Cleere, H. (eds.), *The Crafts of the Blacksmith*, Ulster Museum, 1985

Smyth, A.P., *Celtic Leinster*, Irish Academic Press, 1982

Stead, Ian, Burke, J.B. & Brothwell, D. (eds.), *Lindow Man: The Body in the Bog*, British Museum Publications, 1986

Stead, Ian, *Celtic Art in Britain before the Roman Conquest*, British Museum Press, 1986

Thomas, C. (ed.), *The Iron Age in the Irish Sea Province*, Council for British Archaeology, 1972

Tierney, M., The Celtic Ethnography of Posidonius, *Proceedings of the Royal Irish Academy*, Vol. 60C, 1960

Turner, R.C. and Scaife, R.G. (eds.), *Bog Bodies: New Discoveries and New Perspectives*, British Museum Press, 1995

Twohig, E.S. and Ronayne, M. (eds.), *Past Perceptions – The Prehistoric Archaeology of South-West Ireland*, Cork, 1993

van der Sanden, Wijnand, *Through Nature to Eternity: the bog bodies of northwest Europe*, Amsterdam, 1996

Waddell, J., From Kermaria to Turoe? in Scott, *Studies in Early Ireland*
The Quest of the Celticization of Ireland, *Emania* Vol. 9, 1991

Warner, R.B., The Broighter Hoard: a reappraisal, and the Iconography of the Collar, in Scott, *Studies in Early Ireland*
Cultural Intrusion in the Early Iron Age: Some Notes, *Emania* Vol. 9, 1991

Wood-Martin, William, *The Lake Dwellings of Ireland*, Dublin and London, 1886

PICTURE ACKNOWLEDGEMENTS

Black and white picture credits
Don Sutton Photo Library pp 8, 85, 106, 130; Peter Costello pp14, 15, 16, 21, 22, 16, 91, 119, 121; Bord Fáilte – The Irish Tourist Board pp 17, 60 (top), 89; AKG London, by Erich Lessing; pp 23, 31, 34, 36, 46, 47, 55, 61, 64, 117, 123; Routledge p 25; British Museum pp 43, 44, 45; Professor Barry Raftery pp 49 (painting by Peter Connolly), 59, 71 (drawing by Roy Cooper and Jenny Preece. Courtesy of *Sunday Times*), 72 (courtesy of Liam de Paor), 82-3; Hull and East Riding Museum, Kingston upon Hull City Museums Galleries and Archives p 51; Dennis Coutts, Lerwick, Shetland Islands p 52; National Museum of Ireland pp 63, 65, 76 (top), 92, 96, 100 (top), 102, 104, 105, 107, 108; with kind permission of the trustees of the Ulster Museum pp 67, 103; Silkeborg Museum, Denmark p 75; Department of Arts, Culture and the Gaeltacht pp 87, 109; Cambridge University p 88 (photograph by J.K. St Joseph); Historic Scotland p 93 (top); Susan Hayes drawings pp 93, 113; Navan at Armagh, The Navan Centre, Armagh p 81; From *Muir's Historical Atlas*, London 1911 p 40.

Colour picture credits
Don Sutton Photo Library pp 1 (by Robert Vance), 5 (top) (by Robert Vance); Provincial Museum of Drenthe, Holland p 2 (top); AKG London, by Erich Lessing p 2 (bottom), p 4 (right), p 6 (top), p 7, p 8 (bottom); Archäologisches Landesmuseum, Schleswig p3; National Museum of Ireland p 4 (top left), p 6 (bottom); Bord Fáilte – The Irish Trade Board p 5 (bottom); Silkeborg Museum, Denmark p 8 (top).
Cover photograph: AKG London, by Erich Lessing

INDEX

THE IRISH FAMINE
An Illustrated History

Helen Litton

'As a short intellient overview of 1845–50,
it will be hard to surpass.' *RTE Guide*
'The best documented study, with first-hand accounts and
up-to-date studies.' *Cork Examiner*
'Highly recommended.' *In Dublin*

This is an account of one of the most significant – and tragic – events in Irish history. The author, Helen Litton, deals with the emotive subject of the Great Famine clearly and succinctly, documenting the causes and their effects. With quotes from first-hand accounts, and relying on the most up-to-date studies, she describes the mixture of ignorance, confusion, inexperience and vested interests that lay behind the 'good *v* evil' image of popular perception.

Here are the people who tried to influence events – politicians like Peel, public servants like Trevelyan, Quaker relief workers, local committees, clergy and landlords – who wrestled with desperate need, and sometimes gave up in despair. Why did millions of starving people seem to accept their fate without rebelling? Why was there starvation on the very shores of seas and rivers plentifully stocked with fish?

This is a story of individuals such as Denis McKennedy – dying in Cork in 1846 because his Board of Works wages were two weeks late – and of a society in crisis. It should be read by anyone who seeks a fuller understanding of the Irish past.

Helen Litton took her Master of Arts degree in History at University College Dublin. She is a leading Irish reseracher, editor and indexer.

ISBN 0-86327-427-7

THE IRISH CIVIL WAR
An Illustrated History

Helen Litton

'The illustrations are many and fascinating, the text...lucid and informative in its own right. '
Irish Times

The Irish Civil War has inspired passion, hatred and idealism long after the Free State Army took control in 1923.

In this concise history Helen Litton recounts the events leading up to the signing of the Treaty, the impassioned Dáil debates which followed, the destruction of the Four Couts and the confused fighting of the Civil War itself.

Here are the personalities – the pragmatism of Arthur Griffith, the charisma of Michael Collins, the resounding rhetoric of de Valera, the military tactics of Liam Lynch. Here also are the women of the Cumann na mBan, and the war-weary civilians who had just begun to rebuild their lives from the ashes of the War of Independence.

Using newspaper reports, speeches, eyewitness accounts, and a mass of illustrative material, Helen Litton describes the mixture of confusion, inexperience and sometimes misguided vision that characterised both the Provisional Government and those commanding the Irregulars. From a maelstrom of divided families and divided neighbours a new Ireland had to emerge.

In the style of Helen Litton's highly acclaimed history of the famine, *The Irish Civil War: An Illustrated History* provides a stimulating rethink for all who know the period well, and an informative introduction for those who want to understand it for the first time.

ISBN 0-86327-480-3

THE BOOK OF TARA

Michael Slavin

'This book should inspire young and old to immerse themselves in the fable and fact of what is surely Ireland's most historic sites.'
Peter Harbison, *Irish Times*

Seat of the High Kings, sacred in Irish myth, site of St Patrick's confrontation with the druids – Tara is the heartland of Ireland's Celtic past, the place where legend and history meet. Since before history began, Tara has been at the centre of Irish life, and its power to stir our hearts has never faded: in the 1798 Rebellion it was the rallying point for the United Irishmen, and in the nineteenth century Daniel O'Connell the Liberator relied on its symbolic power to draw a record attendance to a Home Rule meeting. The Hill of Tara – still crowned by the ancient Stone of Destiny, which cries out when touched by a true king – is the keystone around which thousands of years of Irish history and legend have been built.

Michael Slavin weaves together strands of mythology, history, archaeology and geology to recapture a shining and glorious past. Part history, part legend, part walkabout guide, this lavishly illustrated book will thrill any reader with an interest in Ireland and the Irish, past or present.

ISBN 0-86327-507-9

LITERARY TOUR OF IRELAND

Elizabeth Healy

'A passionate, intimate and often illuminating book.'
Irish Times

Elizabeth Healy's route-by-route guide reveals a land which has for centuries inspired poets and storytellers. This lovingly written and informative book conveys the sense of depth and echo that comes from a knowledge of Ireland's richly textured land and literature.

Yeats and Lady Gregory are our guides to the Sligo hills and their mythological presences. We meet Synge in Wicklow and O'Flaherty on the Aran Islands, O'Connor in Blarney Street, Cork and John Hewitt at his home on the Antrim Coast – a host of voices, including our greatest tale of all, the ancient *Táin*. Belfast greets us in the poetry of Ciaran Carson and the footsteps of Seamus Heaney bring us around Mossbawn. We view the villages where Goldsmith gambled and drank away his youth, and befriend the penniless poets of the 'Hidden Ireland' whose exquisite Irish verse is still echoed in modern song and story.

In Dublin with its myriad of literary streets and fictions are Wilde, Shaw and Swift, O'Casey, Joyce and Beckett – pouring words upon its cityscapes before we finally enter Healy's beloved Liffey, *plurabella*, to complete a rewarding and exciting series of travels.

Elizabeth Healy is a former editor of Bord Fáilte's Ireland of the Welcomes.

ISBN 0-86327-446-3

Available from bookshops or direct from:
WOLFHOUND PRESS
68 Mountjoy Square
Dublin 1. Tel: (01) 8740354